Deal with Your Debt

Deal with Your Debt

The Right Way to Manage Your Bill$ and Pay Off What You Owe

Liz Pulliam Weston

PEARSON
Prentice
Hall

An Imprint of PEARSON EDUCATION

Upper Saddle River, NJ • New York • London
San Francisco • Toronto • Sydney • Tokyo • Singapore
Hong Kong • Cape Town • Madrid • Paris • Milan

www.ft-ph.com

Library of Congress Cataloging-in-Publication Data

Weston, Liz Pulliam.
Deal with your debt : the right way to manage your bills and pay off what you owe / Liz Pulliam Weston.
p. cm.
ISBN 0-13-185675-8
1. Consumer credit. 2. Debt. I. Title.
HG3755.W44 2006
332.024'02--dc22

2005015344

Publisher: *Tim Moore*
Executive Editor: *Jim Boyd*
Editorial Assistant: *Susie Abraham*
Development Editor: *Russ Hall*
Director of Marketing: *John Pierce*
International Marketing Manager: *Tim Galligan*
Cover Designer: *Sandra Schroeder*
Managing Editor: *Gina Kanouse*
Project Editor: *Christy Hackerd*
Copy Editor: *Gayle Johnson*
Senior Indexer: *Cheryl Lenser*
Senior Compositor: *Gloria Schurick and Specialized Composition, Inc.*
Manufacturing Buyer: *Dan Uhrig*

PEARSON
Prentice
Hall

© 2006 by Pearson Education, Inc.
Publishing as Prentice Hall
Upper Saddle River, New Jersey 07458

Prentice Hall offers excellent discounts on this book when ordered in quantity for bulk purchases or special sales. For more information, please contact U.S. Corporate and Government Sales at 1-800-382-3419 or corpsales@pearsontechgroup.com. For sales outside the U.S., please contact International Sales at 1-317-581-3793 or international@pearsontechgroup.com.

Printed in the United States of America

Second Printing, September 2005

ISBN 0-13-185675-8

Pearson Education Ltd.
Pearson Education Australia PTY, Limited.
Pearson Education Singapore, Pte. Ltd.
Pearson Education North Asia, Ltd.
Pearson Education Canada, Ltd.
Pearson Educatión de Mexico, S.A. de C.V.
Pearson Education—Japan
Pearson Education Malaysia, Pte. Ltd.

In memory of my mother, Penny

Contents

Acknowledgments

Over the years, thousands of readers have sent me their questions, concerns, and comments about their debts. Many laid bare the intimate financial details of their lives to help me better understand their anxieties, frustrations, and confusion about credit issues. I wasn't always able to help or even respond because of the volume of mail I receive, but I'm deeply grateful for every reader who made the effort to reach out. This tidal wave of information has profoundly affected the way I cover debt and, I hope, helped make this book a more relevant guide for all consumers, whether they're drowning in bills or just looking for a little guidance.

This book also benefited from the help of generous experts in various fields, including Gerri Detweiler of UltimateCredit.com, Diane St. James of ABC Mortgage Consulting, Michael O'Brien of financialaid.com, as well as the folks at Bankrate.com, CardRatings.com, Edmunds.com, and Cars.com among many, many others.

Some of the concepts that wound up in this book were first explored in my columns for MSN Money, and I thank my terrific editor, Richard Jenkins, for his help and guidance.

Applause is also due the excellent team at Pearson Prentice Hall who skillfully guided this book to publication, including Executive Editor Jim Boyd, Development Editor Russ Hall, Copy Editor Gayle Johnson, and Project Editor Christy Hackerd. I owe particular thanks to reviewer Cynthia Smith for her thoughtful comments and questions.

Finally, a big bouquet of thanks to my husband Will, the world's best cheerleader.

About the Author

Liz Pulliam Weston is an award-winning, nationally-syndicated personal finance columnist who previously authored the book, *Your Credit Score: How to Fix, Improve, and Protect the 3-Digit Number that Shapes Your Financial Future* (Prentice Hall 2004).

Liz is one of the most-read columnists on MSN Money and author of the question-and-answer column "Money Talk," which appears in newspapers throughout the country, including the *Los Angeles Times*, the *Cleveland Plain Dealer*, the *Palm Beach Post*, the *Portland Oregonian*, the *Newark Star-Ledger*, *Stars & Stripes*, and others. You can find some of her most recent columns on her Web site, www.lizweston.com.

She appears weekly on CNBC's "Power Lunch" and has been interviewed on numerous other television and radio programs, including NPR's "Talk of the Nation" and "All Things Considered," American Public Media's "Sound Money," and NBC's "Early Today."

Liz is a graduate of the certified financial planner training program at University of California, Irvine. She lives in Los Angeles with her husband and daughter.

Introduction

If you're picking up this book, you're probably concerned about your debts.

If so, you're in good company. Half of Americans in a December 2004 Associated Press poll said they worried about what they owed, with 42% saying their debts caused them "a great deal" of stress. One in five said they obsessed about what they owed most or all of the time.

Some people have good reason to worry. They've maxed out their credit cards, or struggle with an unaffordable mortgage, or face repossession of their car. One in 10 Americans in the AP poll said they had missed a minimum payment in the past six months[md]a sure sign of major credit trouble.

If you're one of those folks, you'll find plenty of information in this book to get you back on your feet.

But you don't need to have overdosed on plastic to be concerned about your debt situation. Most people get little if any education about the right ways to acquire and manage borrowed money. They rely on lenders, family, friends to tell them which loans are "good" or "bad" and to advise them how much they can afford. Many veer between extremes, thinking debt is evil one minute and the next applying for yet another new department store card to get that 10% discount.

The typical book on debt, meanwhile, focuses almost entirely on how to pay it off and ignores when debt might actually be beneficial to your overall financial life.

In reality, debt can be an enormously helpful financial tool, allowing us to buy homes, get educations, and build businesses. Instead of sucking us dry, it can help give us the cash flow we need to grow our long-term wealth. But we need to know how to get it, when to get it, how much to get, and when it's time to pay it off.

This book is designed to help you identify which debts are toxic to your financial health and which actually help you get ahead. You'll learn the smart ways to deal with your debt, including which loans you should pay off and which you should keep. You'll discover how to manage your finances and your credit so that you'll be able to borrow all the money you need at the best rates and terms. In short, you'll be able to craft a sensible, workable plan to achieve your goals and truly deal with your debt.

So let's get started!

1

Isn't Debt-Free the Way to Be?

Debt isn't the root of all evil—but sometimes it sure feels that way.

If you're struggling to cover your bills and are being hassled by collectors, you may curse the day you applied for your first credit card. If you're straining to make minimum payments that feel like maximums, you may swear you'll never borrow again. If you've just graduated with massive student loans, you may question why you ever thought going into debt for education was a good idea.

Even if you've got your bills under control, you may fret about the interest you're paying to some faceless lender or worry that some setback—a job loss, illness, or divorce—could sink your financial ship.

Many books about debt agree with you that owing money is awful, terrible, wicked, and something to eradicate as soon as you can. The authors recount how many dollars are wasted each year on interest payments, and they use anecdotes of people who lost their homes, their marriages, their health, and their peace of mind to too much debt.

They're right that debt when mishandled can be as corrosive as cancer. But the usual prescription is to pay off everything as quickly as possible and learn to live debt-free. The message is enforced with testimonials from people who overcame mounds of bills and who are proud that they live entirely on cash, no longer owing anyone a dime.

Unfortunately, this approach may not be realistic, and it can easily backfire.

Debt Isn't the Enemy

People with serious debt problems may try to do too much too fast and then give up in despair. Or they might pay off the wrong kinds of debt, stranding themselves with too little flexibility to survive a financial crisis. In their zeal to pay off debt, some people neglect other important goals, such as saving for retirement, a home, or college, and ultimately end up hundreds of thousands of dollars poorer than they might have been.

Worse yet, they might be encouraged to continue fighting a battle they simply can't win.

If you're having debt problems, you need information, advice, and a clear-eyed assessment of your financial situation so that you can make the best choices for yourself and your family. Short-term fixes and inspirational slogans might help, but you shouldn't choose them at the expense of your long-term economic health.

Even if you're not in a crisis, it will help you enormously to view debt for what it is: a financial tool that's virtually essential for building wealth, reaching your goals, and living happily.

Think about it. Few of us could afford a home without taking on a mortgage, and many couldn't swing college educations without the help of a few loans. Consider the payoffs:

- The massive growth of the mortgage industry has helped boost the U.S. homeownership rate to nearly 70%, compared to less than 44% in 1940. That, in turn, has helped millions of families get richer: The median net worth for homeowners in a recent Federal Reserve study was $171,700, compared to just $4,800 for renters.

- Student loans helped more than 50 million people attend college, an investment in their futures that pays off in higher incomes and greater productivity. One study found that college graduates usually recouped the cost of their education, including the earnings they missed while attending school, by the time they were in their early 30s.

Debt also can help you survive a job loss, buy a safe car for your growing family, or even start a business—and sometimes all three.

I was raised by a mother who hated debt. She taught me to pay off my credit cards in full every month (thank you, Mom!) and to live within my means. I inherited her distrust of lenders to the point that, after my sophomore year at a small Northwest college, I turned down Stanford University's offer of admission as a transfer student because its financial aid package consisted entirely of loans rather than scholarships or grants.

Imagine my surprise, then, the first time I heard a financial planner tell a client that debt wasn't necessarily bad.

The advice was part of a "money makeover" feature I was writing for my newspaper. The planner suggested our makeover subject invest in her retirement plan rather than rushing to pay off her low-rate student loan debt. The idea that debt repayment needn't always be a top priority was news to me.

Later, I would consult with planners who routinely suggested that their clients open home equity lines of credit to supplement their emergency funds. I had always thought that home equity was sacrosanct, but these planners—smart, objective folks at the top of their field—pointed out it could also be a tool.

I'm glad I got that education because a few years ago my husband and I were able to put it to use.

My husband, who works in the animation industry, was laid off during a massive corporate downsizing that put 4,000 artists out of work. It was several months before he found another full-time job.

Just when our emergency fund was hitting a low ebb, Microsoft approached me about leaving my job at the *Los Angeles Times* to write for MSN. The money was great, and I could work from home—but because I would be forming my own corporation and MSN would be a client, there would be a three-month gap before I got my first check.

Oh, yes, and right after I decided to take the leap, I discovered I was pregnant.

Now, many in the anti-debt crowd would have told me not to leave my job—that it was too great a risk. I took it, though, and we lived on credit cards until those first checks started coming in. After our daughter was born, we used our home equity line to purchase a safer car.

Just a few years later, our income has soared. The credit cards have long since been paid off, and the car borrowing will be retired soon. Debt gave us the flexibility to seize an opportunity that might otherwise have passed us by.

When "Good Debt" Isn't

Debt clearly has a place in our economy and in our lives. That's what many financial gurus are trying to get across when they divide debt into "good" and "bad" categories. Typically, mortgages, student loans, and borrowing to start a business are considered good; most other borrowing is considered bad.

But that leads to another problem with typical debt advice, since too much "good" debt can sink you just as deep as too much "bad" debt.

I've received countless e-mails from people who borrowed $20,000, $50,000, and even more to attend college, only to find that they can't get a job in their field or make even the minimum payments on what they owe. Many had no clear idea of how much their borrowing would cost them when they graduated; they just knew that lenders were eager to give them the cash and that their educations were supposed to help them get ahead.

Furthermore, student loans are almost never wiped out in bankruptcy court, so they can be an albatross that hangs around your neck for life.

Charles borrowed more than $100,000 for his education, but a divorce caused him to drop out of his doctoral program before he got his PhD. He found a job paying $40,000 a year, and his lender agreed to reduce payments based on his income. But his debt is still accruing interest.

"My loan just keeps getting bigger and bigger," he wrote. "I have no hope of paying [it off] unless I win the lottery."

Mortgages are another area where people can quickly get in over their heads.

Many people assume, incorrectly, that a bank wouldn't lend them more money than they could comfortably repay. In fact, lenders know that you'll move heaven and earth to pay your mortgage, even if it means you don't have enough money for other goals, like retirement or vacations.

The reality is that you need to know your own debt limits based on your individual situation and goals.

Which Debts Should You Tackle First?

Then there's the issue of how to prioritize your bills. Often borrowers are advised to figure out which of their debts have interest that's tax-deductible, and to pay those last. They're told to concentrate on paying off the highest-interest-rate, nondeductible debts they have, while paying the minimum on other debts. Once the high-rate debt is paid off, they're told to apply the same payments to the next-highest-rate debt, in a process known as "snowballing."

In some cases, though, it can make more sense to pay a lower-rate debt first, or even a deductible debt before a nondeductible one.

Ginny owed $30,000 in student loans at 5% interest as well as $35,000 on her home equity line of credit, which hovered around 4%. Her income was too high to deduct her student loan interest, but her credit line payment was a write-off. The conventional wisdom would have her pay the student debt first.

But student loans have a feature not common to most other debt: You can get a forbearance (a temporary suspension of payments) that allows you to skip payments while you're unemployed. Since Ginny works in an unstable industry, she resolved to pay down the home equity line first so that she could use the freed-up amount of credit again in an emergency.

The key to managing your debt wisely is knowing which debts are helpful to you and which will leave you worse off. You need to figure out how much debt you can realistically take on so that you don't swamp your financial ship. You need to know when to accelerate your payments and when to pay the minimum. In short, you need to look at debt as a key part of your financial plan, rather than as a scourge that can and should be erased from your life.

Ultimately, being debt-free is a great way to be. But you want to get there the smart way.

Why Debt Management Sounds Strange

The idea of managing your debt rather than eradicating it is foreign to many people. If you have Depression-era parents or grandparents, you may have heard their tales of once-wealthy folks losing everything because of debt. In those days, lenders could "call" loans at will, demanding immediate repayment. As the economy crashed, many did so, meaning that people who had mortgages could face losing their home even if their payments were current.

But the roots of our unease go even deeper. Long before Ben Franklin opined, "So rather go to Bed supperless than rise in Debt," Americans believed there is something shameful about owing money.

In colonial times, excessive debt was a crime that could land you in jail—where you would remain until you, or your family, somehow paid what you owed. More than a few people died of the rampant disease and terrible conditions that typified prisons of that era.

Debtors' prisons weren't outlawed in the U.S. until 1841, and bankruptcy continued to carry a huge stigma until the end of the 20th century.

Of course, our cultural suspicion of debt hasn't kept us from piling up mounds of it. If you know anything about debt in America, you probably know that we owe more than people in any other country, and our pile of IOUs just keeps growing:

- The amount we owe on credit cards and home equity loans has tripled since 1990.

- Household debt burdens have risen to near-record highs, with 20% more of our disposable incomes devoted to debt than was the case 20 years ago.

- The amount and length of the typical car loan continues to increase. In the 1980s, the typical car loan lasted three years; today, 84% of all new car loans last more than four years.

- The average homeowner's equity represents just 55% of the home's value—down significantly from the 65–67% levels that were typical in the decades before 1990. What's remarkable is that equity dropped even as home prices rose spectacularly, indicating that people are putting down less and draining the value from their homes through home equity lending at a furious pace.

It's obvious that some people are overdosing on all this debt. Bankruptcy filings for individuals set new records in 2001, 2002, and 2003 before declining slightly in 2004. Foreclosures in 2003 reached their highest level in 30 years—a remarkable feat considering that foreclosures don't usually rise in a hot real estate market when most homeowners can sell their homes quickly. This indicates that a rising number of homeowners may owe more on their homes than the houses are worth.

Even when people manage to make their payments, the price of debt can really add up over time. The typical homeowner will pay for her house two or three times over by the time she retires a 30-year mortgage. Carrying just $5,000 on your credit cards can cost you $650 a year on average—money that, if invested instead, could grow to $170,000 over your working life. Most people who buy new cars these days are "underwater" as soon as they drive off the lot. They will make payments for years before their car debt is less than what the car is worth.

When Debt Repayment Plans Go Awry

So how could anyone argue that paying off debt is a bad idea?

I can, if you're approaching it in any of the following ways:

You're paying off the wrong debt. In the late 1990s, banks started pushing biweekly mortgage payment plans aimed at helping homeowners pay off their houses faster. By making payments once every two weeks, instead of every month, the homeowner would effectively make one extra house payment a year, shaving years—and thousands of dollars in interest costs—off their loans.

With a $200,000 mortgage at 6% interest, for example, the normal monthly payment would be $1,199.10. By making half that payment ($599.55) every two weeks instead, a homeowner could pay off the home five years early and save $47,282 in interest.

When the stock market started to tank in the spring of 2000, these plans got even more popular. People felt a lot better about "investing" money in their steadily-appreciating homes than they did "throwing it away" on stocks.

The problem with this approach is that many who pursued it were neglecting other financial goals or carrying other, far more expensive debt—including credit cards and personal loans.

The average credit card carries an interest rate of 13% or more, more than twice as high as the mortgage in our example. Furthermore, you typically can't deduct credit card interest on your tax returns. The deductibility of mortgage interest can reduce the effective rate you pay to 4.5% or even less, depending on your tax bracket.

There's something else you should consider—inflation. Most people realize that higher prices gradually erode the value of the dollar, which means many things will cost more in the future than they do today. But inflation also makes debt *cheaper* as time passes. The fixed-rate mortgage payment that seems so onerous today will be much less so in 10 years and might seem almost an afterthought in 30 years.

"Most people don't understand that even modest inflation makes a fixed mortgage payment cheaper every year it's in existence," wrote David, one of my readers on MSN. "My first mortgage, 28 years ago, was $271.60 a month. Had I stayed in that house, I would be spending far more today on my monthly utility bills than my mortgage."

By contrast, money you invest has a chance of beating inflation over time. That means your purchasing power can actually grow, particularly if you invest it in stocks or stock mutual funds. If you're forgoing the chance to invest while you prepay your mortgage, you've really got your priorities backward.

Mortgages are some of the cheapest money you'll ever borrow. Such low-rate, tax-advantaged debt is usually the last kind of borrowing you want to pay off.

You're limiting your financial flexibility. Carlos graduated from college in 1998 with $20,000 in student loans—more than most students at the time, but about average these days. He consolidated his loans to lock in the prevailing 7.455% interest rate. He decided to double his $237 monthly payment to retire his loan faster. Instead of taking 10 years to pay off the balance, he did it in just over five, saving about $5,000 in interest.

Then he lost his job.

If Carlos had put the extra payments into savings instead, he would have had an emergency fund of more than $11,000 by the time he was let go. He could have lived off the cash and asked his student lender for a forbearance while he looked for work. Instead, he had no cash, and his landlord, utilities, and car lender weren't interested in giving him a forbearance; they all wanted their regular payments on time.

By paying off his debt early, he limited his financial options instead of enhancing them.

This issue of financial flexibility has become critical in the last decades as incomes have become more variable, layoffs more common, and bankruptcies a near-epidemic.

Fewer than one in three households in America have enough cash saved to survive more than two or three months of unemployment—and the typical time out of work during a recession can stretch to eight months or more.

An incredible 43% of households have less than $1,000 set aside, according to an analysis of Census Bureau data by SMR Research.

So many families are living paycheck to paycheck that any crisis can tip them over the brink: a job loss, divorce, illness, or accident. (The Bureau estimates that 45 million Americans are uninsured, while millions more are underinsured.)

Instead of focusing single-mindedly on paying off all debt, today's families need to figure out how to put themselves on sound financial footing overall.

You're cutting yourself off from credit entirely. I often receive e-mails from folks who are paying off their credit cards and proudly closing down the accounts once the balances hit zero. They vow to never again use another piece of plastic.

Yet credit cards can be an important safety valve to help families survive job loss or other setbacks. If you don't have enough cash set aside in an emergency fund, you can live on your cards temporarily until the crisis passes.

Furthermore, you generally need to *use* credit to *get* credit. The credit-scoring systems employed by most lenders require you to have and use revolving accounts like credit cards to get the best scores.

Closing accounts can actually hurt those scores and make it more difficult to get future credit. The next time you need a mortgage or a car loan, you could be at the mercy of subprime lenders that charge astronomical interest rates to people with troubled or thin credit histories.

None of this means that you shouldn't learn to live on cash alone while you're repaying your debt. Just don't close the accounts once you've paid them off unless you really and truly can't keep from using them otherwise.

There are certainly people who have completely lost the ability to control their spending. One of them e-mailed me after filing bankruptcy for the third time. He wasn't the victim of bad luck, bad health, or unemployment; he simply spent too much money.

"If I make $150,000, I spend every single dime," he wrote. "What can I do to get my credit back and stop this madness?"

Credit to this man is like booze to an alcoholic. There is no safe way for an alcoholic to have even a single drink, and there may be no safe way for a chronic credit abuser to have plastic.

If that describes you, consider getting help through therapy or a 12-step program like Debtors Anonymous or Overspenders Anonymous.

Most people, however, can survive a credit crisis and move on to responsible credit use.

You're neglecting your retirement savings. One of the pieces of debt advice that most disturbs me is when people are urged to forgo retirement contributions to free up cash to pay their credit cards.

Yes, this will get the cards paid off more quickly—but at what long-term cost?

The problem is that contributions to retirement plans are usually a use-it-or-lose-it proposition. In other words, you can't get back an opportunity to contribute to a tax-advantaged retirement plan once you've let it slip away.

Many employers, for example, will put 50 cents into your 401(k) for every dollar you contribute, up to a certain cap—typically 6% of your salary. If you make $45,000 but don't contribute that 6%, you're missing out on $1,350 of free employer matching money each year. Even worse, you're passing up all the future, tax-deferred growth of your contribution and the employer match.

Let's say you suspend contributions to your 401(k) for five years while you pay off debt. We'll assume that you resume contributions at that time and retire 30 years down the road. If your account earns an average 8% annual return—which, given long-term historical trends, is a reasonable assumption for a portfolio invested 70% in stocks and 30% in bonds—your five-year hiatus could cost you more than $200,000.

You can try to make up for lost opportunities once your debt is paid off by making bigger payments to your retirement plans. But the amount you can contribute to tax-deferred plans is limited by law and often is limited further by company policy. Even if you could somehow compensate for the contributions you failed to make, you simply can't get back the free money you passed up in company matches, or the value of time in helping your money grow.

Here's another example of how this trade-off works. One of the posters on a message board I monitor at MSN was trying to decide what to do with an extra $250 a month: pay off her car loan or fund a Roth IRA.

Accelerating the payments on her $20,000 car loan would save two years on the five-year loan and save her more than $1,000 in interest, and it's the option many posters on the board urged her to take.

I pointed out that the same money, contributed to a Roth, could grow to more than *$175,000* of tax-free money in 30 years.

This isn't just an academic issue. Saving for retirement is critical, and by all reports most Americans are doing a pretty lousy job. Few of us will have the cushy, traditional pensions that previous generations relied on to fund their retirements, and many of us suspect Social Security won't be much help either. We need to be saving more and starting earlier—not delaying or interrupting our contributions.

You're raiding your retirement funds. Chris and Suzanne in Tennessee have $40,000 in credit card debt and $18,400 in an old retirement plan at Suzanne's previous employer. They want to pull it out to pay off part of their debt. They e-mailed me, asking if this was the right thing to do.

"We have been in debt for many years, and this could help kick-start us in getting out of debt," they wrote.

Most people have at least a vague notion that carrying credit card debt is a bad idea. So when they leave a job and their employer sends them a check for their 401(k) balance, they think they're being responsible by using the money to pay off credit card balances.

But if there's one thing worse than suspending retirement savings, it's raiding what you've already set aside.

Chris and Suzanne would face a tax bill come April 15 for taxes and penalties that will equal one-quarter to one-half of the withdrawal they just received. Furthermore, they're giving up all the future tax-deferred returns that money could have earned. (Figure that every $1,000 you withdraw will cost you $10,000 or more in future retirement income.) What they should do is roll the money into an IRA and find other cash to pay off those credit-card bills.

Otherwise, they're just opting for another quick fix that simply makes their financial situation worse. That kind of approach—grabbing for a short-term band-aid rather than the long-term cure—prevents many people from overcoming their debt problems.

Remember how I said there were worse ways to spend retirement money? I often get e-mails from people asking how they can withdraw money from their retirement funds so that they can pay off their *mortgage* early.

Think about that. They're proposing giving up tens of thousands of dollars in tax-deferred future gains and incurring a fat tax bill, so that they can pay off a low-rate, tax-deductible debt. That's just nuts.

Some people propose a variation on the theme. They understand that withdrawals from retirement accounts are stupid, but they think it's a good idea to borrow from themselves via a loan from their 401(k) rather than continue paying interest to a lender.

The big problem with this approach is that 401(k) loans typically come due if you lose your job. If you can't pay back the money quickly, it can be taxed and penalized as a distribution.

There's something else to consider. If your financial situation really takes a dive, you may be able to wipe out your credit-card debts in bankruptcy. Once you've paid them off with a 401(k) loan, that option is gone.

I also wonder how many folks who use 401(k) loans to pay debts are really covering up a serious spending problem. As long as they can keep shuffling loans around, they may never address the real cause of their financial problems: themselves. Forcing yourself to leave retirement plans for one purpose—retirement—can lead you to find real solutions that will ultimately create, rather than destroy, future wealth.

Your debt situation is hopeless. Like many others, I used to think that most people could avoid bankruptcy if they really tried. Now, after writing about the issue for more than a decade, I'm not so sure.

I've heard from too many people who faced six-figure medical bills or credit card debt that totaled more than their entire year's salary. They could struggle for years and still never pay off what they owe. Some empty their retirement funds, drain their home equity, and scrimp for years without ever making an appreciable dent.

Sure, many of these folks could have avoided the fix they were in. But many were as much victims of bad luck as bad choices. And some made decisions that the rest of us would be hard-pressed to fault.

Paul, a military officer, found himself $70,000 in debt after his wife Debbie was diagnosed with breast cancer. The conventional treatments didn't work, so the couple opted for experimental therapies their insurance didn't cover.

For Paul, there didn't seem to be any choice: Go into debt or say no to the only hope his sweetheart had.

"Debbie didn't survive," Paul wrote me, "but I would do the same again in the same circumstances."

Richard's long slide into bankruptcy started when he was laid off from a defense industry job at age 47.

"I worked hard, was a company man, and did the 50-to-80-hour work-week week after endless week, for years," said Richard, who lives in California. "I soon found, however, that my defense-specific knowledge and skills were nearly worthless in the commercial world."

Richard eventually found work, but not before racking up debts that proved unpayable on his new, lower salary.

Dan and Leah were managing just fine until their young son developed reactive airway disease and landed in the hospital with pneumonia. Dan's employer fired him because he missed too much work while attending to his son; without health insurance, the medical bills had to be paid for out-of-pocket.

"We filed for bankruptcy, and that was very difficult," Leah said. "I remember crying at the courthouse. I felt like such a failure for not being able to take care of our own debt."

Paul, Richard, Dan, and Leah have plenty of company. More than 1.5 million personal bankruptcies were filed in 2004.

What many people find is that bankruptcy isn't the credit-killer it used to be. Although the bankruptcy remains on their credit reports for up to 10 years, the growth of credit scoring and the subprime lending industry means that those who have declared bankruptcy can get credit cards before their cases have even closed, auto loans within a few months, and reasonably-priced mortgages within two years. Those who handle their finances correctly after bankruptcy find that they can restore their credit scores to near-prime status within four years of their filings.

Of course, some people feel such a strong moral obligation to repay their debts—however they were incurred—that bankruptcy is not an option.

Many people, though, are simply ignorant of their alternatives or the true gravity of their situation. If anything, they wait too long before they file, continuing to throw money after impossible debts when they could be using that cash to rebuild their lives.

Bankruptcy court is meant to give people a fresh start while protecting their homes and retirement funds, to prevent them from facing a poverty-stricken old age. Bankruptcy should never be the first choice, but sometimes it's the best of very bad options.

How can you tell if it's the right option for you? In the next chapter, you'll see how to evaluate your financial situation, prioritize your debts, and find the expert advice you may need to make that decision.

Addressing the Ants as Well as the Grasshoppers

I'll never forget the father who wrote to me proudly detailing his progress at becoming financially independent. He and his wife were saving prodigiously for retirement, and they had a fat emergency fund. They decided that their next goal would be to retire their mortgage as early as possible. When he worked the numbers, though, he realized that accelerating the mortgage payments meant they'd have to cut way back on their vacation fund. They had long wanted to take a special trip with their daughter, who was 11. He asked me if I thought it wise to put off that journey until the mortgage was retired.

If you have teenagers, you will probably understand my response to him. Go on the trip now, I told him, while your daughter is still delighted to spend time in your company and you can really enjoy the trip as a family. Before you know it, she'll have all sorts of interests and friends that will make her reluctant to take a long trip with her folks, and then she'll be off to college. Seize the moment and go now. The mortgage will still be there when you get back.

That advice shocked a few folks, who presumed that it's always better to save than to spend. In reality, financial planning isn't about one or the other; it's about both. The hardest part of managing your money can be figuring out the balance between living fully today and preparing for the future.

Most debt advice is aimed at the grasshoppers—people with a "live for the moment" attitude. They wind up paying for every purchase two or three times over, because they put it on their credit cards, pay just the minimum balance, and rack up prodigious interest charges over time.

But we shouldn't forget the many ants out there—people who may be erring on the side of living too much for the future. After all, life is not a dress rehearsal—it's the only one you've got. Make sure you live it along the way.

Debt-Free Is the Way to Be—Eventually

Although debt has its place, I'm not among those who believe that it's always better to use "other people's money." These folks advocate having a mortgage as long as you live because you can almost always invest the money at a higher rate of return than you're paying.

That may be true, but there's a strong psychological advantage to being beholden to no lender in retirement, when your income will likely be fixed and your ability to survive financial setbacks may be lessened. Knowing that their house is paid for helps a lot of older folks sleep soundly at night.

Summary

Let's review some important concepts that will guide you throughout this book:

- Debt is a tool that, if handled properly, can help you create wealth.

- "Good" debt can sink you as quickly as "bad" debt; you need to determine your own limits.

- Mortgage debt is some of the cheapest money you'll ever find and is usually the last debt you'll want to pay off.

- The order in which you should pay off other debt depends on your individual situation and goals—not one-size-fits-all advice.

2

Your Debt Management Plan

The last chapter showed you how most advice on debt is too simplistic. People are often encouraged to pay off the wrong debts, in the wrong order, and at the expense of other, more-important financial goals.

That advice can lead people to do some pretty financially disastrous things, like prepaying mortgages instead of contributing to their 401(k)s or stranding themselves without enough financial flexibility to survive a job loss or other setback.

A better approach is to figure out which debts are contributing to your wealth and flexibility and which aren't. Pay off the ones that are endangering your financial well-being and better manage the ones that are increasing your net worth.

But how, exactly, do you do that?

The answer is a three-step plan that helps you understand where you are now, where you want to be, and how best to get there:

- **Get intimate with your debt.** You need to know more than how much you originally borrowed and the monthly payment (which, unfortunately, is all many people remember about what they owe). You need to know your balances on every account, what interest rates you're paying, whether that interest is deductible, when and how the rates can change, and whether you'll face any kind of penalties for paying off an account early.

  You also need some benchmarks, such as what interest rates you *should* be paying and the maximum amount you should carry for each type of debt. You'll find that information, along with a detailed discussion of the advantages and disadvantages of different kinds of debt, in the following chapters.

- **Assess your overall financial situation.** You can't make smart debt management decisions in a vacuum. Your other financial goals, like retirement or college saving, can have a profound impact on which debts you pay off and how quickly. You'll also want to make sure you have enough of a financial cushion to get you through the bad times that can strike any family.

  The discussion in this chapter will get you started thinking about how to prioritize your financial goals, including repaying your debts. As you explore the chapters dealing with each kind of debt, you may refine your plan further.

- **Create your game plan.** Once again, no one debt repayment strategy works for everyone. You need to evaluate your debts, goals, and finances to devise a plan that's smart and workable. The end result probably will look different from the program that would work for your neighbor, your friend, or your brother-in-law. The point is to customize your debt management plan so that it makes the most sense for you and your family. In Chapter 11, "Putting Your Debt Management Plan into Action," you'll create a detailed program that incorporates all your goals. Chapter 11 also has tips for finding the cash to get you to the finish line as quickly as possible.

Okay, let's take these steps one at a time.

Get Intimate with Your Debt

You can get started right now with the first part of this step: knowing exactly what you owe. Dig out your credit card statements and loan paperwork so that you can list all your debts with the relevant details. You can use the form provided in Table 2.1 or a blank sheet of paper. If you're into such things, you can even create your own spreadsheet.

Make sure you include every debt you owe, including

- Mortgages

- Home equity loans and lines of credit

- Credit cards

- Student loans

- Auto loans

- Other bank or credit union loans

- Money owed to check-cashing outfits or payday lenders

- 401(k) or other retirement plan loans

- Debts owed to friends and family

For each debt, write down the following:

- **Current balance owed.** At this point, it really doesn't matter what the original loan amount was; what matters is how far you have to go.

- **Whether the loan is an installment or revolving debt.** Installment debts include mortgages, auto loans, and other debt where you have a set schedule of payments to make and a specific payoff date when the loan is expected to be retired. Revolving debt includes credit cards and lines of credit, where you have a credit limit that you can draw on—and pay off—repeatedly. Paying off revolving debt generally increases your financial flexibility because you can always draw on that freed-up credit line in an emergency. That may not be possible with an installment loan.

Table 2.1 *Debt Repayment Worksheet*

Debt	Lender	Balance Owed	Credit Limit	Interest Rate	Fixed/ Variable	Adjustment Date	Deductible?	Minimum Payment	Typical Payment	Prepayment Penalty?
Mortgage 1										
Mortgage 2										
Home equity line of credit										
Home equity loan										
Student loan 1										
Student loan 2										
Student loan 3										
Student loan 4										
Credit card 1										
Credit card 2										
Credit card 3										
Credit card 4										
Auto loan 1										
Auto loan 2										
Auto loan 3										
Other vehicle loan										
401(k) loan										
Personal loan 1										
Personal loan 2										

- **Current interest rate.** You should find this on your most recent statements, typically listed as your "annual percentage rate."

- **Whether the rate is fixed or variable, and when it might change next.** Credit card rates typically are variable and can change month to month. Installment loans usually carry fixed rates, unless you took out an adjustable-rate mortgage. If you're not sure when the rate is scheduled to change, ask your lender.

- **Whether the interest is tax-deductible.** This is actually more complicated than it might seem, but we'll get to that in a minute.

- **Minimum payment owed.** Again, this is something you'll probably find on your latest statement.

- **Typical payment made.** Ditto.

- **Whether there's a penalty for paying off the loan faster than scheduled.** Prepayment penalties aren't that common. You'll find them on some mortgages and auto loans, but not all. If you're not sure, call and ask.

You can add one more step if you really like to play with numbers by trying to figure out your "after-tax" rate on your tax-deductible debts. Essentially, you need to subtract your tax bracket from the number 1 and multiply the result by the interest rate you're paying.

For example, if you're in the 25% bracket, you'd subtract .25 from 1 to get .75. Multiply that by a 6% interest rate (.06), and your after-tax rate would be 4.5%.

Some folks like to get even more precise and factor in their state and local tax rates as well. Someone in the 25% federal bracket who lives in California may pay an 8% state income tax rate. To figure the effective rate, you multiply the federal rate by the state rate and then subtract the result from the combination of the two rates. This reflects the fact that you can deduct your state taxes from your federal return. It works like this: .25 times .08 equals .02. Add .25 and .08, and you get .33. Subtract .02 from that, and you get .31, so 31% is the combined effective tax rate.

If you enjoy this kind of thing, have at it. But remember that these are still just estimates of what your rate will be over time. Tax rates change constantly, so your tax benefit may be more or less than you think, depending on what's on your tax return in any given year.

Which Debts Are Deductible?

The issue of tax deductibility confounds a lot of people, who assume a loan is either tax-deductible or not. The reality, like so many things in personal finance, can be far more complicated.

Mortgage interest may be tax-deductible—or it may not. Technically, you can write off the interest you pay on mortgages of $1 million or less, as long as you owe the money on your primary residence or a second home. *But if you don't itemize your deductions—and two-thirds of the nation's taxpayers don't—you don't get any tax benefit from your mortgage.*

About half the nation's homeowners get absolutely no tax benefit from their homes—either because they own their homes free and clear or because they're paying too little in mortgage interest and other potentially deductible expenses to justify itemizing. You had to have deductions worth more than $9,700 for itemizing to make sense in 2004 if you were married filing jointly, or $4,850 if you were filing single.

If you're not sure whether you itemize, check last year's return. If you just bought a house this year, you can use TurboTax or another tax program to see if you'll get a tax benefit from your mortgage, or you can talk to a tax pro.

Even if you do itemize, you may be getting only a partial benefit from your mortgage. If your interest payments, property taxes, and other deductible expenses total just $10,000 and you're married, you get an additional tax benefit of just $300. If you're in the 25% bracket, that means all your deductions really saved you only about $75. That's very little tax bang for all the bucks you paid in interest.

Home equity interest is usually deductible. If you itemize, you typically can write off interest on home equity lines of credit or home equity loans, as long as the amount owed is less than $100,000. If you owe more, you can't deduct the interest on the part of loan that exceeds that limit.

Your ability to write off your home equity interest can be limited even more if you fall under Alternative Minimum Tax (AMT) rules. This Byzantine system was originally designed to make sure the wealthy didn't exploit loopholes to escape paying taxes, but today it's snagging many far less affluent families who simply have lots of deductions—usually because they have a lot of kids, they live in high-tax states, or they got certain kinds of stock options from their employers.

AMT rules severely restrict the deductions you're allowed to take, including home equity interest deductions. If you borrowed the money for anything but home improvements—if you paid off credit card debt or bought a car with the money, for example—you can't deduct the interest.

You probably know if you've been hit by AMT rules, but if you're not sure, talk to a tax pro.

Student loan interest probably is deductible. Congress loosened the rules so that married couples with incomes of under $130,000 and singles with incomes of under $65,000 can deduct at least some of their student loan costs (up to a limit of $2,500 a year). (All these figures were accurate as this book went to press, but check with your tax pro, a tax guide, or www.irs.gov for updates.) There's no longer a requirement that the loans be within the first 60 months of repayment. Also you don't have to itemize to take advantage of this deduction—a real plus.

Interest on credit cards and most other debt typically isn't deductible. If you own a business and carry a balance on your business credit card, you typically can write off the interest. People who are self-employed also might be able to deduct some of the interest paid on auto loans for cars used in their businesses.

Otherwise, credit cards, personal loans, auto loans, and other types of consumer debt don't merit a deduction.

You also need to consider one more issue, as discussed next.

Am I Paying the Right Rate?

Most lending these days is based in part on your credit scores, the three-digit numbers that lenders use to help gauge your creditworthiness. Credit scores are a snapshot of your credit picture that tell mortgage lenders, auto finance companies, credit card issuers, and other financial institutions how likely you are to default on your payments. The most-used score is known as the FICO, after its creator, Fair Isaac Corp. (formerly Fair, Isaac & Co.).

Good scores will land you the best rates and terms; mediocre or poor scores can cost you tens of thousands of dollars more in interest over your lifetime.

Table 2.2 shows how much difference even a few points can make on a 60-month $20,000 car loan.

Table 2.2 *Auto Loan Rates by Credit Score*

FICO Range	Interest Rate	Monthly Payment	Total Interest Paid
720–850	5.900%	$469	$2,502
700–719	6.670%	$476	$2,840
675–699	8.634%	$494	$3,723
620–674	10.778%	$515	$4,708
560–619	14.478%	$551	$6,464

Source: MyFico.com and Informa Research

The use of credit scoring has even seeped into areas of your life beyond lending. Insurers use a form of credit scoring to determine premiums, and landlords use scores to determine who gets an apartment and who gets denied. Even employers can make judgments about whom to hire, fire, and promote based on personal credit information.

So much rests on your credit scores that you really need to know what yours are and how to improve them.

You may have heard that U.S. residents are now entitled to one free credit report a year from each of the three major credit bureaus. (You can order your reports at AnnualCreditReport.com or by calling 877-322-8228.) But those reports don't include a free look at your FICO credit scores. For that, you usually have to pay.

The easiest place to get all three credit reports and FICO scores is from MyFico.com, which charges about $45.

The three bureaus (Equifax, Experian, and TransUnion) sells scores to consumers for $7 to $15 each, although sometimes they push their own in-house scores over the FICO scores actually used by lenders. You may also get a free look at your scores by signing up for the bureaus' credit monitoring services.

Since your scores can vary significantly from bureau to bureau, it's best to get a look at all three. But you can get a rough idea of where your scores might fall for free by using the FICO score simulator at Bankrate.com.

Contrary to what you may have heard, checking your own credit reports and scores won't hurt your credit. In fact, it's something you need to do to make sure your reports are accurate and that you're getting the best possible rates and terms.

The following chapters show you what people with credit scores similar to yours actually pay in interest on their loans. Since rates can vary widely over time, you might also want to visit the MyFico.com site and use its Loan Savings Calculator, located in the Credit Education section, to get more up-to-date results for mortgages, home equity lending, and auto loans. Bankrate.com is another good source of information on prevailing loan rates.

If your scores are below 720 or so, you'll want to focus on getting them higher. I wrote a whole book about how credit scoring works and how best to boost your scores—*Your Credit Score: How to Fix, Improve, and Protect the 3-Digit Number That Shapes Your Financial Future* (2004, Prentice Hall). Here's the thumbnail version of the best ways to get your numbers up:

- Fix any serious errors in your credit report, such as accounts that aren't yours or negative information that's more than seven years old (or 10 years old in the case of bankruptcy).

- Pay your bills on time, all the time. Even a single late payment can devastate your score.

- Pay down your debt. The FICO formula likes to see a wide gap between your credit limits and the amount of credit you actually use.

- Apply for credit sparingly.

Exhausted yet? Well, get another cup of coffee because we've just begun.

Assess Your Financial Situation

Every financial plan needs to start with goals: what you really want and are trying to achieve. You may have very specific notions: a trip to Europe in two years, college education for your kids in 10, retirement in 25. Or you may be looking for a state of mind, such as feeling in control, content, and not anxious about money.

The real work of financial planning comes when you try to figure out which goals are most important, how to prioritize them, and how to save for them while paying the expenses of your day-to-day life.

Setting you up with a full-fledged financial plan is well beyond the scope of this book. But you must address two goals before you construct any debt repayment plan—retirement savings and financial flexibility.

Retirement Savings

This needs to be a high priority for almost everybody. It should take precedence over just about every other goal—including your child's college fund.

This is really tough for many parents to hear, since they're so focused on providing a better life for their kids. One of my personal finance professors put it this way: If worse comes to worst, your kid can always borrow money for school. No one will lend you money for retirement.

In the past couple of decades, the burden of ensuring an adequate retirement has shifted from the employer to the worker. Instead of traditional defined benefit pensions, which promise a set paycheck in retirement to loyal employees, companies increasingly offer defined contribution plans like 401(k)s. How much money workers will have to spend in retirement depends on how much they contribute and how well they invest the money. The company makes no promises.

Another change is in the works. Most retirees today get half or more of their incomes from Social Security. But Social Security has already promised far more benefits than it can deliver to future generations. Higher taxes or cuts in benefits may be needed. If the system is privatized, more risk will be shifted to workers.

Finally, we're living longer than ever before—and that means living longer in retirement. Many Americans plan to cope with the high costs of retirement by working longer. More than half of the workers (54%) surveyed by the Employee Benefit Research Institute in 2004 expected to work to 65 or older, while 68% expected to work at least part-time in retirement.

But, as the EBRI noted, the typical worker retires at age 62, and four out of 10 retirees it surveyed said they left work earlier than they'd planned—often due to ill health, disability, or layoffs.

All these issues underscore the need for most of us to stockpile a decent amount of money—and the earlier we start, the better.

The value of time in helping our savings grow really can't be overstated. Even relatively small delays in getting started, or brief interruptions along the way, can have an outsized impact on how much we can put away.

The Value of Starting Early—and Not Stopping

To illustrate this point, many financial planners use the example of the twins. One twin puts $3,000 aside in a Roth IRA starting at age 22. She continues contributing $3,000 annually until age 32, and then she stops—never to contribute another dime.

Her sibling, in contrast, doesn't start contributing until age 32 but continues until they both retire at 62.

Who has more money? The answer may surprise you: the first twin. She accumulates $437,320, compared to her sister's $339,850 (assuming that both siblings earn an average 8% annual return). The first twin's early contributions gave her a head start that her sibling couldn't match.

This illustration shows why it's important to get an early start; now here's one to show why it's important to keep going.

Let's say our siblings each put $10,000 into a 401(k) annually starting at age 22. Ten years later, the second sibling stops contributions for five years to pay off some debt; the first sibling continues funding her 401(k).

Once she restarted her contributions, how much would Sibling Two have to shell out annually to catch up with her sister by retirement age? The answer: $15,496 a year, or 55% more each year than she would have had to contribute if she hadn't stopped. She'll need to make those extra payments for 25 years to match her sister's kitty at 62.

There's another reason not to stop. Many people who suspend retirement contributions have a tough time resuming their savings later, just as those who put off getting started often let inertia keep them on the investing sidelines. We can always find other ways to spend our money once we've got our hands on it; that's why most of us are far better off simply putting our retirement contributions on automatic and not stopping, whatever the short-term temptations.

That doesn't mean we should tolerate high-rate debt in our lives or delay paying it off indefinitely. The better solution is typically to find money for debt repayment by cutting other spending, not by shortchanging our retirement savings.

You'll notice that I use the words "typically," "normally," "usually," and "generally" quite a bit. That's on purpose because most rules have exceptions, and the rules of debt repayment are no exception.

If any of the following are true, you may be able to suspend your retirement savings for a while so that you can pay off your most troublesome debt faster:

- **You work in a job that offers a traditional defined-benefit pension plan that will give you 50% or more of your salary in retirement.** This is likely to be true if you're a public-school teacher, police officer, firefighter, or federal government worker—and you plan to retire in the job rather than switch to the private sector. State and local governments often have such generous pension plans as well. These plans are far rarer among private companies; if you're not sure what you've got, ask your human resources department.

- **You know how much you need to save for retirement and are on track to *exceed* that goal.** If this is true, you're a rare bird indeed, since most people have never done the calculations needed to determine how big their retirement fund should be—and many fewer are actually saving more than necessary. If this describes you, though, you have some flexibility to redirect part of your retirement contributions to another goal.

- **Your employer doesn't offer a 401(k) or similar plan or doesn't offer a match.** People who fail to contribute when there is a match are passing up an instant 50% return (if the company matches 50 cents of each dollar you contribute). Unless you've fallen into the clutches of a payday lender, the interest rates you're paying on your borrowing are much, much less. You can see how it's foolish to give up a 50% return to pay off a debt that's costing you 10%.

If you don't have a tax-deferred retirement plan at work, however, or the one you have has no match, you're not giving up the "free money" match if you don't contribute. That doesn't mean you shouldn't start saving at some point—and the earlier the better—but you're not costing yourself as much by not contributing as someone who has a decent plan.

Financial Flexibility

Retirement isn't the only factor you'll want to consider as you construct your debt repayment plan. You'll also want to make sure your household can survive the financial catastrophes that can wait around almost any bend.

As mentioned in the previous chapter, we Americans are pretty lousy at saving for a rainy day. Fewer than one out of three households have the cash on hand to survive even a short stretch of unemployment, and more than 40% live paycheck to paycheck. This helps explain the soaring bankruptcy rate and the state of financial stress in which many people live.

Unfortunately, traditional debt repayment plans ignore how close to the edge most people live. They typically advise paying off the highest-rate debt first, even if doing so could make you more vulnerable to financial setbacks.

A few fortunate folks don't have to worry about their financial flexibility quotient—they've got plenty of cash to tap in an emergency. If you can answer "true" to any of the following three statements, you're one of the lucky few who don't need to make financial flexibility an immediate goal:

- You have six months' worth of expenses saved in a safe, liquid, and easily-accessible place like a money market or savings account.

- You have less than six months' worth of expenses saved in cash, but you have ready access to a similar amount of cash on credit cards or a home equity line of credit.

- You have friends or family who are well-off and who would gladly lend you enough money to pay the bills for six months.

   (Personally, I wouldn't advise anyone to rely on the kindness of others to survive a job loss or other financial setback—especially if your borrowing would cause your lender financial hardship. But if you have the proverbial rich aunt or doting parent who would step in if necessary, you already have more financial flexibility than most people.)

As I noted in the previous chapter, most people can't answer yes to any of these questions. But you still may not need to make emergency savings a high priority if you can answer "true" to *all three* of the following statements:

- Your household has more than one income earner.

- You work in a growing industry where the possibility of lay-offs is remote.

- You have adequate life, health, and long-term disability insurance and enough cash to continue your coverage for at least six months if one or both income earners lose their jobs.

If all three are true, you should still boost your emergency savings eventually, but it needn't be one of your highest priorities.

Save or Pay Off Debt First?

Again, most people aren't in the enviable position of having financial flexibility to spare. And what many want to know is: Should I hold off on my debt repayment plans until I get my emergency fund pulled together, or should I pay off my debts first?

The question of whether to save or repay is one that people with a little financial savvy love to debate. The save-firsters point out that the more cash on hand you have, the better you can survive an emergency without running up more debt.

The problem with that approach is that many people would be paying pretty high rates on their debt while they slowly put together their cash stash. And it usually doesn't make much sense to earn 2% or so on your savings when your debt is costing you 10%, 15%, 20%, or even more.

I'm of the school that urges people to pay off their credit card debts before they do anything else. Credit cards usually carry pretty high rates, and every dollar of credit card debt you pay off frees up a dollar of unused credit space on your cards that you can use if you face a real emergency. Unused credit on cards and a home equity line of credit can serve as a de facto emergency fund until you get around to saving for a real one.

The key, of course, is to stop using your cards while you're in debt repayment mode unless you're facing a real emergency. You can't crawl out of the hole you're in if you keep digging.

Paying down revolving debt like credit cards and lines of credit can have another beneficial effect: It can quickly boost your credit score, the three-digit number lenders use to help gauge your creditworthiness. Among other things, the credit-scoring formula measures the gap between the credit you're using and your available limits; the wider you can make that gap, the better. Paying down debt is a great way to strengthen your score and put you in a good position to get low rates the next time you need a loan.

Case Studies

By now, you're beginning to grasp how complex figuring out the right debt repayment plan can be. We'll use two fictional characters, Stefano and Ingrid, as examples to explore further the necessary trade-offs people need to make when figuring out their plans of attack.

Stefano and Ingrid have many financial details in common: They both have a mortgage, a student loan, an auto loan, and credit card debt. Both have a child they want to send to college, and both are somewhat behind in saving for retirement, although they're contributing enough to their workplace 401(k)s to get the full company match. Yet their situations—and debt repayment plans—are quite different.

Stefano is married; he and his wife both work outside the home. They both feel reasonably secure in their jobs and have considerable equity in their home that they could tap in an emergency.

Stefano's student loan rate is relatively high because he consolidated his loans when rates were near their 8.25% cap. His auto and credit card rates are low at 5% each, however, thanks to his excellent credit score.

Ingrid's credit, by contrast, is pretty mediocre, thanks to the devastating effects of her divorce. The single mother drained most of the equity in her home to pay off the debts from her marriage, and she has almost nothing in savings. Her auto and credit card rates are in the double digits, thank to her middling credit scores. The good news is that her student loan rate is low, since she consolidated when rates were hitting bottom.

Ingrid has poor financial flexibility because her household has only one income, little savings, and no home equity. Her plan is as follows:

1. Save one week's salary (that's gross, or before taxes and deductions, not after) in a money market or savings account. This fund should help her meet unexpected expenses so that she can stop using her plastic while she pays off her credit card debt.

2. Pay off the cards, starting with the highest-rate card first.

3. Once that debt has been paid down and her credit score has improved, refinance the auto loan to a lower rate.

4. Boost emergency savings to an amount that equals three months' expenses.

5. Boost retirement savings until she's on track for retirement.

6. Increase emergency savings to an amount that equals six months' expenses.

Paying off the car and student loans isn't a priority, since the repayments wouldn't enhance her financial flexibility. She couldn't, in effect, get the money "back" that she paid into these debts. That's a sharp contrast to payments on a revolving debt like credit cards; usually every dollar you pay down is a dollar that you can borrow again in an emergency.

(Okay, technically she could get another loan against her car, but the amount would be reduced from her current balance since the value of her car would have dropped considerably by the time she got it paid off.)

You'll notice something else isn't a priority: her child's college fund. Until her own retirement and emergency savings needs are met, she shouldn't be investing money for someone else.

Of course, once she's on track with savings and retirement, she may very well decide to put aside some money for college—or she might choose to retire the auto loan and start saving for her next car. What she probably won't accelerate are payments on her student loan, which is a cheap and flexible debt to have.

Now let's look at Stefano's plan. Although he's in a much more secure financial situation, he too must juggle multiple priorities. His student loan is his highest-rate debt at 8.25%. His credit card rate is fixed at 4.99% for the next few months, but it likely will rise after that. Meanwhile, he needs to have at least some money on hand so that he's not in the position of charging auto repairs or other predictable expenses to either his credit cards or his home equity line of credit.

Stefano's first step is like Ingrid's: Put aside some cash. After that, it's quite different:

1. Save one week's salary (that's gross, or before taxes and deductions, not after) as cash for emergency expenses.

2. Boost retirement savings by funding a Roth IRA.

3. Pay off the credit cards.

4. Simultaneously begin increasing emergency savings while paying down the student loans.

5. Once the emergency fund has three months' worth of expenses, raise retirement contributions until he's on track for retirement.

6. Begin contributions to his child's college fund.

Some would be appalled at the idea of increasing retirement contributions when credit card debt is outstanding. But funding a Roth is a use-it-or-lose-it proposition, and Stefano's good credit score means that he'll most likely be able to find another relatively low rate even if his current card goes up.

Still, Stefano knows it isn't wise to have credit card debt indefinitely, even at single-digit rates. The balance on his cards is money he can't access in an emergency, and it leaves him vulnerable to all the various tricks credit card companies like to pull on their customers (for more on these shenanigans, see the next chapter).

Stefano's student loan, by contrast, is a relatively benign debt. The interest is tax-deductible, reducing its real cost, and Stefano can temporarily suspend or reduce his payments if he loses his job.

The student loan debt also is big enough that it will take years to retire, even if Stefano devoted all his available cash to paying it off. Stefano doesn't want to wait that long to have a three-month supply of cash on hand, which is why he wants to start pursuing both goals at the same time.

Stefano also has no plans to retire his auto debt. He figures his college fund contributions will earn greater returns than what he's paying for the loan.

The choices Stefano and Ingrid made may be right for them and wrong for someone else. People have to weigh their goals, understand their situation, and choose a path that makes sense to them.

Create Your Game Plan

By now you have at least a rough idea of how you want to prioritize your goals, including which debts you'll pay off first. To complete your game plan, two more steps remain: locating the cash to fund your plan and making sure you're paying the lowest rates possible so that you can get to the finish line faster.

Chapter 11 goes into more detail about the various places you can find cash. But here's a list to get you started thinking:

- What could you sell? Unloading an unneeded vehicle could raise some significant cash (and lower your auto insurance premium as well). Or maybe you could auction that Hummel collection on eBay. Perhaps you could hold a yard sale to simultaneously reduce your clutter and boost your bank balance.

- Where can you cut? Almost every budget has some fat. Many families spend a big chunk of their disposable income on groceries and dining out, two areas that are very easy to trim. Gym memberships are usually a big waste of cash. Or you can cut back to basic cable, or drop the service altogether. Remember, the deeper you slice, the quicker you'll be out of debt. If you need more ideas, check out one of the many frugality-oriented Web sites like The Dollar Stretcher (www.stretcher.com) or a book like Amy Dacyczyn's *The Tightwad Gazette*.

- Can you pick up more income? Maybe you're overdue for a raise at work or can temporarily add a second job. Now is probably not the time to launch a risky, cash-eating side business, but some people can turn their hobbies into money-makers (by selling handiwork, for example) or start low-cost service businesses walking dogs, running errands, or house-sitting.

Getting your interest rates down will save you money as well. The following chapters have specific information about the best ways to reduce your rates on the major categories of debt, such as credit cards, mortgages, auto loans, and student loans.

Should You Pay Off Your Debt with More Debt?

You may be tempted to implement a more sweeping solution by using a home equity loan, a cash-out mortgage refinance, or a debt consolidator or by borrowing from a workplace retirement plan to lower your rates or your payments.

In some situations, these loans make sense. All too often, though, these solutions make matters worse.

For one thing, these loans usually turn what should be short-term debt into long-term debt. You could end up paying more in interest than if you had just paid off the cards out of your current income.

If you haven't addressed the basic problem that got you into troublesome debt, you could just be digging the hole deeper. Most people who use home equity lending to pay off credit cards, for example, run up new credit card debt within a few years. *The wealth they should be building with their homes is instead being drained away forever.*

Using home equity lending or a cash-out refinance has another problem. Normally, credit cards, medical bills, and personal loans can be erased in a bankruptcy filing if your financial situation really goes south. Pay them off with mortgage debt, though, and you've just secured them with a loan that can't be wiped out.

The same is true of retirement plan loans. Most 401(k)s, 403(b)s, and other workplace plans are protected from creditors' claims in bankruptcy court if you should have to file.

Withdrawing money from a 401(k) has another downside: You lose out on the tax-deferred returns that your money could earn in the plan if you left it alone. Every $10,000 you take out of a 401(k), for example, could cost you $100,000 or more in future retirement income, assuming it had been left alone to grow at an 8% average annual rate for 30 years. And if you lose your job, you typically must repay the loan within a few weeks, or you'll owe penalties and taxes on the balance.

Again, this doesn't mean you should never tap your home equity or retirement. You'll learn guidelines for when and how to do it right in upcoming chapters. Just don't turn to it as your first resort until you read up on all the potential disadvantages.

Debt "Solutions" to Avoid

One kind of loan you can probably strike off your list is an unsecured debt consolidation loan, where a company offers you a loan not secured by an asset like your house.

The fees for this kind of lending are typically outrageous, and the loans usually just stretch out your payments, ultimately costing you much more than if you'd paid off the original debt. That's if you get the loan you apply for at all; this area is rife with fraud and phony come-ons designed to part you from whatever money you have left.

You should approach debt negotiation or debt settlement with extreme caution as well. The companies offering these services typically promise to settle your debts for pennies on the dollar, but such settlements can devastate your credit score. That's if you get any service at all; sometimes fly-by-night outfits just disappear with your fee. If you really can't pay what you owe, bankruptcy is often a cleaner solution.

"Debt elimination" shouldn't even be on your list because it's an outright fraud. The criminals running this scam pretend that you can eliminate your obligation to repay your mortgage, credit cards, or other debt by using a "certificate" they provide—usually for a fee of $2,500 or more. They use all kinds of ridiculous arguments about the legitimacy of the Federal Reserve system, and sometimes they throw in a quote or two from the Constitution, but it's all bunk. What you get is a worthless piece of paper that, if you actually try to use it, will trash your credit, allow the bank to foreclose on your house, and perhaps put the FBI on your tail for trying to defraud a financial institution.

If You're Already Drowning

Most of what you've read so far is directed at anyone who's concerned about debt. But if your concern has already escalated to fear or outright panic—if you no longer can pay the minimums on your debt, or collection agencies are already calling—you need to take some extra action right now.

The following game plan is adapted from my previous book, *Your Credit Score*, in the chapter on dealing with a financial crisis. It consists of three basic steps:

1. Figure out how to free up some cash.

2. Evaluate your options.

3. Choose a path and take action.

Step 1: Find the Cash

You have two choices—cut expenses or increase income. You may need to do both.

You also may need to go beyond the easy cuts—fewer dinners out, dropping the gym membership—to more substantial changes. Even your so-called "fixed" expenses, like your mortgage or rent, aren't really set in stone.

I'm not saying you'll have to move. But you should at least identify all the potential savings available to you. You may find it helpful to break those savings into three categories:

- The easy stuff: expenses that you could ditch with little effort

- The harder stuff: expenses that would require more sacrifice to trim

- The last-ditch stuff: expenses you would cut only as a last resort

Step 2: Evaluate Your Options

This step actually includes a number of other tasks, all of which take a little time but that are essential to making sure you choose the right option.

Task 1: Prioritize Your Bills

Don't let bill collectors tell you what debts are most important. You're the one who needs to decide.

Divide your bills into three categories: essential, important, and nonessential. Essential bills are the ones that, if you didn't pay them, there would be catastrophic consequences (see Table 2.3).

Table 2.3   *Essential Bills*

Bill	Consequence for Not Paying
Mortgage or rent	Foreclosure or eviction
Home equity loans or lines of credit	Foreclosure or eviction
Groceries	Starvation
Utilities	No lights, heat, water, or phone
Payments on a car needed for work	Lost job
Essential medical treatments	Death or serious illness
Child support	Jail

Important bills are the ones that you should pay if at all possible, since failure to pay them would have serious consequences. Table 2.4 gives some examples.

Table 2.4   *Important Bills*

Bill	Potential Consequence
Income taxes	Wage garnishment, loss of tax refund
Court judgments	Wage garnishment
Student loans	Wage garnishment, loss of tax refund
Loans secured by property you want to keep	Repossession of property
Auto insurance	Loss of license, fine
Medical insurance	Catastrophic medical bills

Nonessential bills include debts that aren't secured by property. Failure to pay these debts could have serious repercussions for your credit score and may eventually result in lawsuits and judgments. But skipping these payments won't put you out on the street:

- Credit cards

- Department store cards

- Gas cards

- Medical bills

- Legal bills

- Personal loans

- Loans from friends or family members

You may have other bills not mentioned here; use your best judgment to categorize them.

Once you've got your list, go back and fill in two more columns:

- The monthly payment you typically make

- The minimum monthly payment you need to make to stay current

Task 2: Match Your Resources to Your Bills and Debts

Look at the first two categories of savings you identified in Step 1—the easy stuff to cut, and the harder stuff. Then add those to your monthly net income (what you get in your paycheck after all the taxes and other deductions have been taken). Now compare that income to your first two priorities—essential bills and important bills. Can you cover the minimums required? (See Table 2.5.)

Table 2.5   *Essential and Important Bills*

Essential/Important Bill	Typical Payment	Minimum Payment
Mortgage		
Home equity		
Groceries		
Utilities		
Car payment(s)		
Medical treatments		
Child support		
Income taxes		
Court judgments		
Student loans		
Other secured debt		
Auto insurance		
Medical insurance		
Other		
		Total minimums:

   If you can't cover the minimums, you may have some options before opting for last-ditch cost-cutting measures. It's frequently possible, for example, to get a forbearance on your student loans or to negotiate payment plans with the IRS. The first you can do yourself, usually just by talking to your lender; for IRS help, you're probably best off using a tax pro. Even child support can be reduced if you prove to the court your financial situation has worsened, but this can take a while and may require a lawyer's help.

   Other possibilities: You could sell stuff or take that second job we talked about earlier. You could increase your paycheck by eliminating or reducing 401(k) contributions *temporarily* or, if you regularly get a tax refund, by reducing your withholding.

If you still can't pay for the essential and the important, you'll probably need to take a last-resort action, such as selling your house or renting cheaper digs. You'll also need to consult a bankruptcy attorney about wiping out any nonessential debts, since those obviously won't get paid.

If you've got your bases covered and have money left over, however, you're ready for the next task.

Task 3: Figure Out a Repayment Plan

Many calculators on the Web can help you create debt repayment plans; I like the Debt Reduction Planner at Quicken.com. Similar tools are available in personal finance software, such as Quicken and Money. For now, don't include your mortgage or the other top-priority bills we covered in the previous task. You're just trying to design a plan for nonessential debts with the money you have left over after paying your more important bills (see Table 2.6).

Table 2.6 *Nonessential Bills*

Nonessential Bill	Typical Payment	Minimum Payment
Credit cards		
Department store cards		
Gas cards		
Medical bills		
Legal bills		
Personal loans		
Loans from family/friends*		$0
		Total minimums:

*If the worst consequence of missing payments is a chilly reception at Thanksgiving dinner, you should probably suffer that rather than stiffing your other creditors.

First, see how much progress you can make with the increased income you identified; then add in the lump sums you've estimated you could raise by selling stuff. Finally, check out how fast you could get out of debt if you took some of those last-ditch options.

You also could consider—carefully—using a home equity loan or line of credit to pay off your cards. But read Chapter 11 closely before you do.

In the best-case scenario, you'd be able to retire your credit card and other unsecured debt in less than five years without too much strain. If you still have good credit scores, you may even be able to convince your lenders—just by asking—to lower your interest rate so that you can get the debt paid off faster. You might even be able to get them to waive some late fees and other penalties. Credit card companies are often eager to give their best customers a break, rather than risk losing them to competitors.

What if your lenders won't cooperate, and you can't quite pay the minimums they're asking? At this point, you might want to consider contacting a credit counselor—but choose carefully, and understand the risks.

Credit counselors can help you negotiate repayment plans that lower or waive your interest charges. While these debt repayment plans by themselves don't affect your FICO score, lenders' reactions to the plans may well have a negative impact on your credit. Your current lenders might report you as late, since you're not paying the full amount owed, and potential lenders might view your repayment plan as equivalent to Chapter 13 bankruptcy.

Also you have to watch out for wolves in credit counselors' clothing. The Federal Trade Commission has found that some companies masquerading as nonprofits were charging hidden fees, lying to clients, and channeling business to their for-profit affiliates. If you go this route, you'll want to stick with agencies affiliated with the National Foundation for Credit Counseling at www.nfcc.org.

If even that route doesn't work—you can't get your credit cards, personal loans, and medical bills paid off within five years—seriously consider consulting a bankruptcy attorney.

Step 3: Choose Your Path and Take Action

If you can pay off your unsecured debts without help, or with the help of home equity borrowing, you should cut up your credit cards right now. "What?" you might be saying. "Cut up my cards? How can I live without my cards?" News flash: People do it all the time.

If you have easy access to your cards, you'll keep using them. Your credit cards need to be off limits until you're debt-free. Debit cards with Visa or MasterCard logos are accepted at most places that take credit cards; the difference is the money comes directly out of your checking account, so it's much tougher to overspend.

You don't need to actually close your credit card accounts, which could potentially hurt your score, unless you really have an otherwise uncontrollable spending issue.

If you need a credit counselor's aid, make the appointment to get it done. Every day you delay costs you more in interest and puts off the moment when you'll be debt-free.

If bankruptcy is the best of bad options, file. Some people would like to see a return to the debtors' prisons that were a feature of American life until

1841. As it stands, however, being unable to pay a debt is not a crime. The bankruptcy laws were designed to give people a fresh start. If you've done your best to find money to pay your bills, but you've failed, you shouldn't shun this option.

Summary

Before we move on, let's review some key points from this chapter:

- You need to know all the relevant details about your debt before you can properly manage it.

- The rates you pay on your borrowing depend heavily on your credit score.

- Retirement savings and financial flexibility need to be a key part of most people's financial plans, even when—*especially* when—they're paying off debt.

- Some common "solutions" for debt, such as borrowing against home equity and tapping retirement accounts, often make matters worse.

- If you can't pay off unsecured debts like credit cards and medical bills within three to five years, you may need to consider bankruptcy.

3

Credit Cards

Some people view credit cards the way prohibitionist Carry Nation viewed alcohol: a hideous evil visited upon an unsuspecting and easily duped public.

It's true that credit cards have paved many a road to financial ruin. The soaring bankruptcy rate attests to that, as does the fact that millions carry credit card balances at rates so high that they would have been illegal just a generation ago. There's no question that some people would be better off without plastic. Many others would have a lot more cash in their pockets if credit card companies weren't so fiendishly creative at finding ways to snatch it away.

But just as most people can have a cocktail without ruining their lives, most people can handle a credit card or three. The oft-repeated statistic that Americans carry an average of $9,000 in credit card debt is actually bunk (more on that later). A large group of credit card borrowers (about 40% by most estimates) use cards solely for convenience, charging balances that they pay off in full each month.

Credit cards provide protections that simply aren't available if you pay by cash or check. The credit card company serves as a middleman if you have a dispute with a merchant, and it can even help you replace purchases that are lost, broken, or stolen. (If you have a gold or platinum card, check the benefits guide that came with it. Chances are you'll be pleasantly surprised at the perks you'll find.)

If someone steals your card or uses your account number without permission, you're typically not liable for a dime. (Most issuers waive the $50 fee they could legally charge.) Then there are all the rewards you can rack up with the right card—cash back, free flights, upgrades, hotel stays...even merchandise.

Credit cards can provide an important safety valve in a nation that's pretty much forgotten how to put aside a little money for a rainy day. If you don't have enough cash to survive a few months of unemployment—and two out of three households don't—you can live on your cards for a while until you land your next gig. It's not the best way to survive a financial crisis, of course, but it can work.

When people get in trouble is when they let credit cards tempt them into living beyond their means.

Some credit card issuers allow their borrowers to pay 2% or less of their balances each month. That means people can carry towering amounts of debt without really feeling the pain—at least not directly.

At 2%, the typical minimum payment on $5,000 of credit card debt is only about $100 a month. At 13% interest (which is about average as this book went to press), you would need *27 years* to pay off the balance—and you'll wind up paying for everything you bought twice over when you count in the interest you've paid.

At a 19% rate, that same debt would take you *54 years* to retire, and you'd pay for everything more than *four times*. (These figures are courtesy of Marc Eisenson, author of *The Banker's Secret*.)

Imagine paying for everyday purchases for literally decades. Every dinner you've long since digested, every toy that broke years ago, every household gadget or piece of clothing that's been donated to the Salvation Army— all paid for four times over.

Now, imagine that instead of sending that $100 a month to a credit card company, you invested it instead. Over your working lifetime, you could rack up a nest egg of nearly $350,000, assuming your investments earned an average 8% annual return.

That's a pretty steep price to pay for the "convenience" of not paying off your balance.

Carrying a balance also leaves you vulnerable to the many different ways credit card companies have devised to ding their customers, from rates that soar overnight to sneaky balance-transfer fees. (Again, you'll consider lots more on that in a minute.) If you don't carry a balance, you don't have to care when your issuer cranks up your rate—because you're not paying interest anyway.

Aren't there exceptions? You might have been led to think that any type of debt is okay, as long as you don't overdo it and you manage it correctly. But that's not true when it comes to credit cards.

Credit card debt is simply corrosive. Much of the time, it's ridiculously expensive, and even when it's not (listen up if you've received low-rate balance-transfer offers), it encourages people to spend more than they make, which is never a good financial habit to acquire.

People who play the balance-transfer shuffle—moving their debt from one card to another in search of low rates—do themselves a particular disservice. All those accounts can ding your credit score, as can moving money from one card to another with a lower credit limit. Do it long enough, and you may find that your score has suffered enough that the low-rate offers suddenly dry up, stranding you with a big debt on a card that's about to jack up its rate.

PLAYING THE BALANCE-TRANSFER SHUFFLE

The proliferation of 0% transfer offers has tempted a lot of people to play some pretty interesting games with their debt.

Jonathan in Los Angeles bragged to me that he has plenty of money in his savings account to pay off his $5,000 credit card debt. But he'd been bouncing the debt from one 0% offer to the next while earning about 2% on his savings. Wasn't that smart?

Not when you think about it. The 2% interest Jonathan earns translates into about $100 a year. Since he's in the 25% federal tax bracket, he loses $25 of that "windfall" to federal taxes and another $8 or so to state taxes. That leaves $67, or about $5.58 a month in "profit."

For that small return, he has to pore over each deal's fine print to make sure he doesn't get tripped up by some gotcha like balance-transfer fees. He has to make sure he gets every payment in well ahead of the due date, or he risks triggering a sky-high penalty rate. He has to know exactly when the offer expires and search out and secure the next offer in time.

Jonathan could make the same "return" for a lot less effort by merely skipping his ritual latte-and-muffin habit one day a month, or by buying one less drink at the local watering hole.

And he wouldn't be risking his credit score playing the balance-transfer game. Each new account he applies for dings his score; so does transferring a balance from a higher-limit card to a lower-limit one. Jonathan's been making matters worse by closing out the old accounts; closing accounts never helps your score, and can hurt it.

If you decide to grab one of these low-rate teasers, watch the fine print. Credit card issuers increasingly are hiding tricks and traps in the fine print that are catching even veteran balance shufflers. Russ in San Antonio told this cautionary tale:

"I am one of those who continuously rolls credit card balances to new cards before the teaser 0% interest term limit approaches. I have been enjoying 0% interest for several years. Within the last few months, something happened that has never happened before. I applied for a new card balance transfer. I was eventually approved. When I received my statement, my very first invoice included an 'over-limit' fee.

"Just in case that did not immediately hit you, look at it this way. I apply for a card, not knowing the amount of the credit limit that will be granted. The card company transfers the balance amount I requested, but it makes my credit limit slightly less. The card company gets an over-limit fee along with a transfer fee. I did call the company, and they waived the over-limit fee, but it makes me wonder how many folks are paying without challenging something like that."

Carrying credit card debt is not the norm in America, despite what we're frequently told.

Most Americans owe nothing to credit card companies, according to detailed figures compiled by the Federal Reserve Bank in its Survey of Consumer Finances. One quarter of U.S. households don't have any cards at all, and another 30% or so regularly pay off their balances in full.

Of the households that did carry a balance, the median amount owed was $1,900. That means half of the households with a balance owed more, and half owed less.

So where did we get the idea that the average American is $9,000 in hock? That idea is actually a misquote of a real but easily misunderstood statistic.

CardWeb.com, which tracks credit card trends, divides the total outstanding credit card debt at the end of each year by the number of American households that have at least one credit card (see Table 3.1).

Table 3.1   *Credit Card Debt by Household*

Year	Average Debt
1990	$2,966
1991	$3,103
1992	$3,275
1993	$3,646
1994	$4,301
1995	$5,213
1996	$5,875
1997	$6,247
1998	$6,618
1999	$7,031
2000	$7,842
2001	$8,234
2002	$8,940
2003	$9,205

Source: CardWeb.com

If you know anything about statistics, though, you probably know that averages can be incredibly deceiving.

Need an example? Imagine yourself in a room with nine friends—and two of those friends are Bill Gates and Warren Buffet. The *average* net worth of a person in that room would be more than $8 billion, even if the rest of you are flat broke. Gates and Buffet are so mind-bendingly rich that they skew the average.

A similar phenomenon seems to be happening with credit card debt. Most folks don't have any, and most of those who do don't have much. But a few folks have a lot, and that skews the average. (That and the fact that CardWeb's statistics include balances that are about to be paid off, as well as those that are carried month-to-month.)

The continued misuse of the CardWeb statistic does a real disservice to people with credit card debt because it can mislead them into thinking that they're the norm—that carrying debt on plastic is how you're "supposed" to live your life. Nothing could be further from the truth.

In fact, if you want to achieve financial independence one day—that is, if you ever want to retire or have enough money to chart your own course—you need to learn this lesson. While you're at it, teach it to your kids:

Pay off your credit card balances in full every month.

The only exception, as I've noted, is when you're experiencing a true financial emergency like a job loss. In that case, you'll want to preserve your cash.

Running out of cash before you run out of month isn't an emergency. That's just overspending. If you encounter that situation, go into savings overdrive to come up with the cash to pay your cards. Sell something. Eat beans and rice. Bike to work to save gas. Do whatever it takes to get in the habit of relentlessly, religiously paying off your credit card bill.

Of all the financial lessons my mother taught me, this was one of the most important. My mother was so dead set against paying credit card fees of any kind that when her Visa card first introduced an annual fee, she cut up the card and sent the shards back to the bank. (Within a few weeks she received a new card with the fee waived—and a letter of apology.)

Not owing credit card debt has freed me in so many ways. When I was first starting out, I had more money than many of my peers to save for retirement and spend on the things I enjoyed, including travel. When the newspaper I was working for in 1992 abruptly shut down, I learned that I had enough cash saved—and my expenses were so reasonable—that I could easily survive for a year without touching my retirement savings. While others panicked, I had the luxury of figuring out what I wanted to do next and even turned down a few jobs before I found the one I wanted. Now that's freedom.

Our Love Affair with Credit

Unfortunately, it's a freedom many people don't know. Even though most Americans appear to be handling their debt just fine, a significant—and growing—number of people are in serious trouble. Consumer bankruptcy filings have more than doubled since 1990, as shown in Table 3.2.

Table 3.2   *Bankruptcy in America*

Year	Total Nonbusiness Filings
1990	718,107
1991	872,438
1992	900,874
1993	812,898
1994	780,455
1995	874,642
1996	1,124,286
1997	1,349,510
1998	1,405,695
1999	1,281,360
2000	1,217,628
2001	1,451,789
2002	1,566,358
2003	1,624,677
2004	1,563,145

Many condemn this trend as a symptom of a "live for today" ethic or on baby boomers who never learned the meaning of delayed gratification.

The truth is a little more complicated.

Many consumer bankruptcies are precipitated by medical bills. That's not surprising, given that 45 million Americans are uninsured, and others face hefty copayments and caps on their coverage as employers struggle to contain burgeoning health-care costs. One study at Harvard University suggests that as many as half of all consumer bankruptcies are caused by medical bills.

Lack of savings and significant credit card debt are other factors that can tip a family over the edge into bankruptcy, particularly when they face a financial setback, like a job loss or divorce.

People also can get into trouble when they use their personal credit to launch or maintain a small business. One out of three new businesses fail within five years, according to the Small Business Administration, and many take their owners' credit with them.

FLOATING A BUSINESS ON YOUR CREDIT CARDS

So many small businesses are launched on personal credit cards that a few cautionary words are in order.

That's because people who would never think of carrying a balance for "frivolous" personal spending often will max out their cards trying to keep their business afloat. They may view their money-losing enterprise the way a parent views a sick child: They'll do anything necessary to keep the loved one alive.

But businesses *aren't* children, and people who can't make sensible decisions about their companies may find themselves in bankruptcy court.

Take Dee. She launched her restaurant with a small pile of cash, a few credit cards, and a lot of hope. She was prepared for the business not to break even right away—perhaps too prepared.

The location she picked didn't turn out to be as terrific as she thought. Her expenses mounted much faster than she expected. She needed every dollar she earned, and then some, to buy supplies and pay her employees.

Pretty soon her cards were maxed out, and she couldn't even pay the minimums. She filed for personal bankruptcy.

She refused to shut down her business, however. She was convinced that with a little more advertising and a little more time, she could make her restaurant viable. She started borrowing money from friends, family, and even the business's landlord. She fell behind with tax payments to the IRS and to her state. Her checks to suppliers started bouncing so often that one by one they refused to deal with her at all. One morning she couldn't open the restaurant because there wasn't enough food to serve.

Once it was all over, Dee confessed, "I was like a junkie looking for the next fix. Anywhere I could get money to borrow, I would. I just didn't want it to fail."

It was an expensive lesson. Dee's personal credit has been trashed. The bounced checks mean she's pretty much black-listed from having a checking account for five years. Her retirement funds are drained, and she owes more than $14,000 to various people and the government.

I don't want you to abandon your plans to be an entrepreneur. But go into business with your eyes open. Here are some thoughts:

- **Create a business plan.** You need detailed research on your market, your competition, and your expected revenues, among other factors. You can find books to help you at your local library, or visit the Small Business Administration's Web site at www.sba.gov.

- **Look for small-business funding.** Once you have a written plan, you may be able to convince a lender to give you a long-term, low-rate small-business loan.

- **Decide in advance how much to borrow.** If you must use your cards to start your business, set a limit on how deep you'll go into debt. Avoid using more than 50% of your available credit on any card.

- **Have an exit strategy.** Your research should give you a good idea of when you can expect to break even. If you haven't done so by your target date, pull the plug.

The explosion of available credit has had a profound affect on who has debt and how much they carry. For years, credit card issuers and other lenders were pretty cautious about how much credit they would extend, and to whom. It wasn't until the U.S. Supreme Court essentially nullified state caps on interest rates in 1978 and Fair Isaac introduced its first credit bureau-based score in the mid-1980s, that card issuers got more confident that they could properly manage the risks involved in extending more credit to a wider group of people. Now that they could charge essentially any rate they wanted, the credit card companies figured they could take on riskier clients—and make them pay proportionately for the greater chance of default they presented.

Table 3.3 shows how credit card charging soared in the 1990s and beyond.

Table 3.3 *Credit Card Use*

Year	Credit Card Charges	Growth
1990	$172.6 billion	18%
1991	$188.8 billion	9%
1992	$201.8 billion	7%
1993	$232.3 billion	15%
1994	$285.5 billion	23%
1995	$358.1 billion	25%
1996	$411.6 billion	15%
1997	$443.7 billion	8%
1998	$454.3 billion	2%
1999	$490.1 billion	8%
2000	$568.5 billion	16%
2001	$607.7 billion	7%
2002	$660.9 billion	9%
2003	$683.4 billion	3%

Source: CardWeb.com

This explosion in credit affected everyone—not just the baby boomers. More than 80% of college students these days have credit cards, and they graduate with an average of $2,000 in credit card debt, on top of nearly $20,000 in student loans.

Credit troubles are affecting older Americans as well. As a matter of fact, people over 65 were the fastest-growing group of bankruptcies in the 1990s, as shown in Table 3.4.

Table 3.4 *Changes in Bankruptcy Filings by Age of Filer*

Age	1991	2001	Change
Under 25	98,974	94,717	–4%
25–34	417,510	464,647	11%
35–44	348,115	602,254	73%
45–54	179,745	414,608	131%
55–64	69,395	128,671	85%
65+	23,890	82,207	244%

Source: Consumer Bankruptcy Project

So it's not just the young and naïve or baby boomer spendthrifts. Credit problems can afflict people at any age.

The True Cost of Carrying a Balance

Carrying a credit card balance makes you more vulnerable to whatever setbacks life throws your way. Every dollar you've charged is a dollar you can't access in an emergency, and your card issuers want at least their minimum payments, regardless of whether you have a job. Credit card debt might not be the primary reason most people file for bankruptcy, but it's certainly a contributing factor in many cases.

If you need more convincing that carrying a credit card balance is a bad idea, let's review a few of the ways credit card companies have devised to part you with your hard-earned cash when you don't pay your balance in full.

Floors But No Ceilings

Most credit cards these days have variable rates that are tied to some short-term rate benchmark, like the prime rate. Theoretically, when the Federal Reserve reduces short-term rates, what you pay on your credit card should drop as well.

But many credit-card lenders have created interest-rate "floors" to protect their profits. The rate can't drop below this minimum, no matter what's happening with interest rates in general. When the Federal Reserve was chopping interest rates during and after the 2001 recession, about one in four credit card rates didn't budge because the rate had already hit its "floor."

While card issuers have limited their "downside," there's really no limit on their "upside"—how much they can charge.

Overnight Rate Changes

Some people think they've protected themselves from the swings and arrows of outrageous rates by opting for a fixed-rate card. In reality, there's no such thing in the credit card world as a "fixed" rate. No matter how iron-clad you think your rate guarantee is, the credit card company can wriggle out of it thanks to the fine print in the application you signed—or in those little brochures the credit card company sent you after you got your card.

Sometimes they really bury the notice.

Jim in Portland, Oregon, received a fat envelope from one of his credit card issuers recently.

"When I opened it, there were multiple inserts, many with large print and colorful graphics, offering anything from Matchbox toy cars to multiple free gifts, where the customer pays only the shipping charges. The smallest insert, with by far the smallest type, was a brochure notifying me of an increase in my [interest rate]. It went on to say that the increase was not due to my account history or behavior. They just decided to make a business decision to increase it to these new terms. When I called the company, they were very vague and couldn't really explain the increase other than 'We have the right to do so.'"

Typically, the card company has to give you just 15 days' notice to change any of the rates, terms, or conditions on your account. If it has already warned you that certain behaviors can spike your rate, the change can happen overnight.

The average "punitive" rate jumps up about 8 percentage points—from 13.9% to 21.9%, for example, although some go even higher; 29.99% isn't uncommon.

Here are just a few of the ways your rate can spiral:

- **You make a late payment on that card.** And "late" is in the eye of the credit card company. You might have mailed your payment a week ago, but if the card company says the check didn't arrive at its processing center, it's considered late. Many credit card companies now have due "times" in addition to due "dates": If your payment doesn't arrive at the center by 1 p.m., it's late, and you get slapped with late fees and a higher rate.

- **You make a late payment on any other card or loan you have.** Credit card companies cruise your credit reports regularly, looking for signs you're getting in over your head on any of your accounts—and punishing you swiftly if they see any red flags. Consumer Action, a San Francisco consumer advocate, says nearly half of all credit cards now have such "universal default" penalties.

- **You consistently make only the minimum payment.** Credit card companies used to like this behavior, since it meant more profits for them, but they've figured out this is often a sign someone is about to default.

- **You max out the card—or any other card.** Again, this is a sign you're getting overextended and may be about to default.

- **You apply for another card or loan.** The card company may decide you simply have too much credit available and jack up your rate to compensate.

Of course, the card issuer's attempt to protect profits can actually make it more likely that an on-the-edge customer will default.

"What do credit card companies think they're accomplishing when they jack up interest rates?" one reader fumed. "If the person couldn't afford to make the payment before, they're sure not going to be able to make it when the rate is 29%."

Rates aren't the only thing the card issuer can alter abruptly. Many people who run into serious financial trouble find that their card companies begin to lower their credit limits—the amount the customer is allowed to charge each month.

Unfortunately, the customers may not notice the changes right away, increasing the chances they'll go over their new, lower limit. Then the credit card company can charge them $29 over-limit fees—and perhaps jack up their rates again.

Fees and More Fees

Over-limit and late fees have become a huge profit center for credit card issuers. In fact, fees now make up about a third of bank revenue, according to R.K. Hammer Investment Bankers. And the bigger the balance you carry, the bigger the fees you're likely to pay.

In the early 1990s, the typical late payment was about $10. Now the average is close to $30, and several card issuers have instituted "tiered" late fees that can push the toll even higher. Those who owe less than $100 might pay $15, while those who owe $1,000 or more might pay $39.

These bigger late fees can be another trap for maxed-out consumers. The late fee can put them over their credit limit, which triggers—you guessed it— an additional over-limit fee. Depending on how much is owed, the minimum payment due might not be enough to pull the borrower's balance below the limit, which means another over-limit fee the next month. It can be an ugly cycle.

Balance-Transfer Roulette

People with good credit often get flooded with offers encouraging them to move their debt to a new card at a temptingly low rate. These offers are typically loaded with booby traps:

- **Rates that go "sproing!"** Most of the rates offered on balance transfers are fairly short-term—three to six months, typically. Then the rate can leap higher than the one you're already paying. You may fully intend to transfer the balance again before that point, but card issuers know that many will forget to switch in time and others may not be able to find a better rate. Even the offers that promise a "low rate for the life of the balance" have tricks up their sleeves, as you'll see next.

- **Balance-transfer fees.** Many lenders tack on a fee equal to 2% to 3% of your balance when you take advantage of their offers. Depending on how long it takes you to pay off the balance, that fee could wipe out any interest rate advantage of the lower-rate card.

- **Higher rates for purchases.** Most cards that offer low balance-transfer rates have much, much higher rates for new purchases. And, importantly, *any payments you make are deducted from the low-rate portion of your balance first.* Your higher-rate debt continues to accumulate interest. Some cards pretend to get around this by offering a low rate for purchases as well, but typically that rate leaps upward after a few months. If you haven't paid off the balance-transfer portion, you start paying big bucks in interest on those purchases.

- **Bait and switch.** This is an ugly and increasingly common ploy: Lenders send you a "preapproved" offer for a great rate, or they advertise the offer heavily on TV, the Internet, and direct mail. Once you apply, though, the lender decides you don't qualify for its best rate and sends you a much higher-rate card instead.

- **Expensive add-ons.** The offers sound tempting: Pay a small fee, and you won't have to make payments if you lose your job, become disabled, or die.

  Although these offers sound like insurance, which would be regulated by the state, they're actually known as debt-suspension or debt-cancellation contracts and are largely unregulated.

They're also ridiculously expensive. The amount card issuers actually pay out, compared to the price they charge for the contracts, is in the 1% to 3% range, said Birny Birnbaum, head of the Center for Economic Justice and a former Texas insurance commissioner.

The restrictions on these contracts are considerable. Your heirs usually get the death benefits only if you die accidentally, rather than of disease or natural causes. The debt suspension works only if you stop using the card—and what consumer can afford to give up his card if he's disabled or unemployed and has less income?

Most people are much better off buying regular life and disability insurance from a reputable company. If you can't qualify for a regular policy, you could consider one of these credit card contracts, but make sure you understand the terms and how the protection works.

- **The incredible shrinking credit score.** As I mentioned earlier, playing the balance-transfer game can damage your credit score, the three-digit number used in most lending decisions. Merely applying for a new card can ding your score; so can transferring a balance from a high-limit card to a lower-limit one. Many people make matters worse by closing out their old cards once their balances are transferred to the new ones. (Remember, closing accounts can't help your credit score, and may hurt it.)

Despite all the ways they can trip you up, balance-transfer offers also can help you climb out of credit card debt if you use them correctly. The key is to focus on using the low rate to help you pay off the balance, instead of as an excuse to continue carrying debt.

Your goal should be to pay off your balance, or as much of it as possible, before the low rate expires. With a $2,000 balance at 0% interest, for example, you'd need to make monthly payments of at least $334 to pay off the balance in the six months these offers typically last. At 4.99%, boost your payments to $338.

Web sites like Bankrate.com and CreditRatings.com also can help you hunt for good offers.

In addition, take the following precautions:

- **Consider alternatives.** If you can't pay off your balance before the introductory rate expires, consider shopping instead for a card with a low, fixed rate. No, you can't guarantee the "fixed" rate won't change, but you *know* the other card's rate will climb—and you don't know whether you'll be able to score another great balance-transfer offer when it does.

- **Know a good rate when you see one.** If your credit is good—your FICO score is 720 or more—you should be able to qualify for rates under 10%. If it's mediocre—in the 650 range—you'll be lucky to pull in a rate in the mid-teens, although the introductory rate may be lower. Not sure what your scores are? You can get a general idea by using the FICO score simulator on Bankrate.com.

- **Scour the fine print.** Find out exactly how long the low rate applies and mark the date on your calendar as soon as your card arrives. Avoid the offers that apply for just a few months or lenders that reserve the right to send you a higher-rate card if you don't qualify for the low-rate offer.

- **Know the fees.** If the card charges a fee to transfer your balance, make sure you'll save enough during the low-rate period to offset the additional charge. Again, the calculators at Bankrate.com can help with the math.

- **Have another card for purchases.** Even if the card boasts low rates for purchases as well as transfers, remember that any balances you owe when the introductory rates expire will start accruing interest at a much higher rate. It's better to have a separate card for new purchases (and to pay those off in full every month).

Gotchas for Those Who Pay Their Balances

Once you get your balances paid off, you can breathe a sigh of relief that you're no longer held hostage to the credit companies' rate games.

That doesn't mean you can lower your guard entirely. Because about 40% of credit card customers pay off their balances in full each month, card companies look for ways besides interest charges to ding them as well.

Late and over-limit fees are the obvious ways credit card companies can still get you, but there are others as well:

- **Cash-advance fees.** There are few more expensive ways of getting cash than using your credit card—loan sharks come to mind. Typically even the lowest-rate cards charge 19% or more when you get cash, and the charges start from the minute you pull out the money. There is no grace period, even if you don't otherwise carry a balance. (The grace period is the time before interest charges accrue.)

- **Less grace.** Speaking of grace periods, those have been shrinking as well. It used to be that if you didn't carry a balance, you had about 30 days from the day your statement closed before you had to pay interest. If you paid within that grace period, no interest charges would be due. Now the average grace period has slipped to 23 days, and sometimes even less; a few cards have no grace period at all, even if you don't carry a balance. (If you do carry a balance, there's no such thing as a grace period; your new charges begin accruing interest immediately.)

- **Conversion fees.** Taking your credit cards overseas used to be a great deal. You'd get the same great exchange rates that big banks get, instead of the lousy rates usually offered to tourists at storefront exchange outfits.

  You can still get those boffo rates, but the advantage has been dulled since card companies charge a 1% to 2% fee on top of the 1% fee typically charged by Visa and MasterCard.

  If you have more than one credit card, you might call and ask your issuers what their currency conversion fees are and take the card with the lowest one. (Frequent travelers recommend taking a backup card as well. Some merchants don't accept American Express, for example, but do take Visa or MasterCard. Also it's smart to call your issuers before you leave and let them know what countries you'll be visiting; otherwise, their fraud-sniffing software could see the overseas transactions as a sign of theft and shut down your ability to use your card.)

The Right Way to Pay Off Credit Card Debt

Hopefully I've convinced you it's time to get rid of those credit card balances. You'll want to review the information in the preceding chapter to make sure you're coordinating your debt repayment plan with other important goals, like your retirement and increasing your financial flexibility.

Your next step should be figuring out if you can minimize your interest rates.

If you have good credit, this might be as simple as calling the credit card issuers to ask for a better rate. You might let them know you've been receiving some mighty tempting balance-transfer offers lately, which is often all the incentive they need to cut you a deal.

If they balk, you actually might use one of those offers to lower your rates. (If you haven't gotten any lately, check for one on Bankrate.com or similar sites.)

If you come up empty or you don't have good credit, consider transferring balances to your lowest-rate cards. Just make sure you're not using up all your available credit; "maxing out" your cards is a good way to trigger a much higher penalty rate. (In fact, using more than about 30% of your limit on any credit card can hurt your score, but you may want to take the temporary ding to speed up your debt repayment plan.)

How about using a home equity loan or line of credit to pay off your balance? Yes, you can get a lower rate that's tax-deductible to boot, but this isn't a good choice unless your finances are otherwise sound and you can commit to not running up new balances. (For more details on the disadvantages of these loans, see Chapters 2, "Your Debt Management Plan," and 5, "Home Equity Borrowing.")

Using a loan from your 401(k) to pay off credit card debts is often a bad idea as well. If you lose your job, the unpaid balance can be penalized and taxed as an early withdrawal, and you lose all the tax-deferred returns you could have earned on the money.

Debt consolidation loans usually just stretch out your payments and jack up your overall interest costs and fees. Credit counseling—where a nonprofit negotiates a lower rate with your credit card companies—can have a negative impact on your credit. You should use it only if you've already fallen behind on your payments.

Most people can create and execute their own debt repayment plans without any outside help.

But you do have to stop using your cards.

There's nothing like living on cash (or a debit card tied to your checking account, which is the next best thing) to help you learn to live within your means.

If your spending isn't totally out of control, you can keep one card for "emergencies" and travel, but only if you commit to paying off the balance in full every month. If you can't do that—and some people can't—go cold turkey.

Now, the perennial question: Which balance should I pay off first?

You'll find a variety of different opinions, depending on which debt guru you consult. Each approach has its benefits and drawbacks:

- **Pay the smallest balance first.** This approach gives you the psychological boost of achieving a zero balance quickly on at least one of your accounts, and that little victory could help you stick to your debt payoff plan. But if other debts are accruing at higher rates, you could wind up paying more in total interest.

- **Pay the highest-rate balance first.** This is probably the most-recommended plan of attack, since you retire your costliest accounts first. But it may take you longer to achieve your first paid-off account, and it may not be the most helpful for your credit score.

- **Pay the balance that's closest to its limit.** If one or more of your cards is maxed out, lenders can use that as an excuse to raise your interest rates—both on the affected accounts and on any others you might have that have a universal default penalty. Paying down these high-balance debts can help your credit score and ultimately contain your total interest costs.

Sometimes it can make sense to use a mix of approaches. You might pay down the card that's closest to its limit first, for example, and then start working on your highest-rate debt.

Whichever account you tackle first, your plan of attack will be basically the same. Pay as little as possible on your other debts, and throw every available dollar at the debt you're targeting.

Once that debt is retired, you can decide on the next debt you want to eliminate and direct your money there, again paying the minimums on your other bills.

By the way, the minimum you need to pay may be slightly more than the amount listed on your monthly statements. As I mentioned, some cards penalize borrowers who consistently pay only the minimum. Before you launch your payoff strategy, call each of your issuers, and ask them if they could invoke a penalty interest rate if you pay only the minimum on their cards or any other cards. If that's the case, add $10 or so to the minimums to keep yourself in the clear.

You can use debt reduction calculators available on many Web sites, including Bankrate.com and Quicken.com, to see how fast your extra payments can retire your debt. Even seemingly small increments can help you toward your goal. Sending an extra $25 a month on a $5,000 balance could trim nearly 16 years off the time it takes to pay back the debt, according to debt expert Gerri Detweiler, and save you more than $3,000 in interest costs.

Table 3.5 demonstrates how fast larger payments can retire a $5,000 balance at different interest rates.

Table 3.5 *Retiring a $5,000 Balance at Different Interest Rates*

Monthly Payment	10%	15%	20%
$100	5 years, 5 months	6 years, 7 months	9 years, 1 month
$200	2 years, 5 months	2 years, 7 months	2 years, 9 months
$300	1 year, 7 months	1 year, 7 months	1 year, 8 months

Another tip: Consider setting up some kind of automatic payment plan so that money is whisked from your checking account to your bills without your having to give it a whole lot of thought. Most people have busy lives and find that with money, the fewer decisions they have to make, the better. You can set up an automatic debit plan that lets the credit card company take a set amount of cash from your checking account each week, or you can set up a recurring payment through your online bill payment system.

A final note: As you pay off your debt, don't ask your credit card issuer to close your cards or lower your credit limits unless you really can't control your spending. Closing accounts or lowering limits can hurt your credit score.

BUILDING—OR REBUILDING—YOUR CREDIT

Whether you're getting your first credit card or trying to recover from a credit disaster, the steps you need to take are pretty much the same:

Step 1: Check your credit report at all three bureaus.

You're looking for errors and outdated information that could keep you from getting credit. Federal law entitles you to one free report from each of the three major bureaus once a year. You can order your reports by calling 877-322-8228 or by visiting www.AnnualCreditReport.com.

You might have a credit report if you've never had credit. Somebody else's information could have inadvertently been included in your file, or you might be a victim of identity theft. If so, you'll want to clear that up before applying for new accounts.

Step 2: Set up checking and savings accounts.

Lenders see these accounts as signs of stability. If you've wound up on the Chexsystem blacklist because you bounced checks, you might visit http://chexsys.tripod.com to find a list of institutions that don't use the system and that might be willing to give you an account.

Step 3: Apply for the right plastic.

If you're a college student with no credit history, you're in luck. There's probably no time in your life when it will be easier to get a regular, unsecured credit card such as a Visa or MasterCard. (Unsecured cards don't require you to make a deposit.) Lenders are willing to take a chance on you before graduation that they may not afterward because they know your parents are probably willing to bail you out of trouble as long as you're in school.

Don't go overboard: Get one or two low-rate, no-fee cards, and use them lightly but regularly. Don't carry balances, and don't even come close to maxing out.

If you can't get a regular credit card, apply for the secured card. Your credit limit will be equal to the amount of cash you deposit with the lender, typically $200 to $1,000. Look for a decent deal: Don't apply for cards that ask for big upfront fees. Find a card that reports to all three bureaus and that converts to a regular unsecured card after 12 to 18 months of on-time payments. Your credit union might be a good place to start, or check out Bankrate.com's list of secured card issuers.

Gas and department store cards are also fairly easy to get. Again, one or two is enough. These cards don't help your credit as much as a bank card (Visa, MasterCard, Discover, and so on), but they're usually easier to get.

Step 4: See if you can "piggyback" on someone else's good credit.

You may be able to build your credit faster if you can convince someone with good credit to add you as an "authorized" or joint user on a credit card.

Being a joint user means that the other person's history with that account is typically imported to your credit report. If the person has paid on time and otherwise has handled the account well, that helps you. But the other person's missteps could hurt you as well, so make sure you pick carefully.

Being an authorized user is a little more iffy; some lenders won't report authorized users to the credit bureaus unless the user is married to the original card holder. If you're hoping to build your credit history this way, call and ask the issuer about its policy.

Another way to piggyback is by finding a cosigner to help you get a loan, which in turn will help build your credit history. If you don't pay, however, your cosigner's credit will suffer.

Step 5: Get an installment loan.

To get the best credit score, you need both revolving accounts (credit cards, lines of credit) and installment accounts (auto loans, personal loans, mortgages). Your credit union might be a good place to start. If you opt for an auto loan, try to make a large down payment so that you can refinance in a year or so when your credit has improved.

> **Step 6: Practice "safe credit."**
>
> Don't just put your cards in a drawer. You need to have and use credit regularly to generate a credit score. Just be careful: Don't charge more than you can pay off each month, or more than 30% of the card's limit. Pay all your bills on time, all the time. And don't go overboard applying for cards and loans; you need only a few accounts to build a good score.

Getting the Right Reward Card

Everybody, it seems, is getting some kind of perk for using plastic: Frequent-flier miles. Cash back. Rebates on cars, free merchandise, hotel upgrades, theme park tickets. Your credit card can even help you save for college or retirement.

This proliferation of perks isn't problem-free, however. Card issuers have complicated their offers immeasurably in recent years by offering scores of ways to earn and redeem your rewards. Use your card at a certain grocery store, and earn more points. Redeem with a certain hotel, and get an extra day free. You get the picture.

That leads to a lot of second-guessing. Do I have the best card? Am I earning the most possible points? What's the best way to spend them?

The answers to all these questions are fairly simple if you carry a balance from month to month. That's because reward cards aren't for you.

Reward cards have interest rates that are consistently higher—often much higher—than you would pay on a plain-Jane card. You might think that since you're carrying a balance anyway, you might as well get the perks, but the finance charges you'll pay will more than offset the value of any goodies you get.

You're better off looking for the lowest-rate card you can find so that you can pay off your debt as quickly as possible. Once you've done that, you can start tackling the confusing world of rebate cards.

The best card depends on a lot of factors, including how much you charge, how much you travel, and how much flexibility you want in earning and spending your rewards.

To get the best deals, you'll need to invest some time in choosing a card and managing it afterward. To get the maximum rewards, you'll probably want to focus your spending on one or, at most, two cards; otherwise, you'll have points scattered (and expiring) hither and yon, with too few on any one program to make much difference.

View your reward program as a kind of investment; the returns typically are commensurate with the amount of time and attention you give. You'll want to pay attention to the statement stuffers or e-mail newsletters that come with your card, since these typically give you tips on earning extra points.

Here's what you need to know to get started:

Know your options. Most people have heard of cards that earn frequent-flier miles and those that offer cash back. Cards that give you future discounts on car purchases or leases are also popular.

But that's barely scratching the surface of what's available today. The Stockback and Nesteggz cards, both offered by MBNA, can contribute 1% to 2% of your spending to your Individual Retirement Account. Cards affiliated with BabyMint or UPromise make contributions to college savings plans. Several issuers have cards that earn rebates on specific types of purchases, like gasoline, or on categories of spending, like entertainment. Disney and Universal have credit cards (issued by Bank One and Chase, respectively) with rewards that can be redeemed for theme-park admissions, DVDs, and movie tickets.

If your goal is earning free travel, you'll have to choose from a wide variety of options:

- **Airline-affiliated cards.** These cards earn you miles on a specific airline, like American or United. If you're a frequent traveler who can concentrate most of your flights on a single airline, these are usually the best option to help you earn free tickets and upgrades.

- **Travel-reward programs.** If you have to spread your miles on different airlines, you might be better off with a card that gives you more flexibility. American Express and Diners Club both have well-regarded plans that allow you to redeem miles on a number of different airlines. Many Visa and MasterCard issuers also have reward programs with miles that can be redeemed on any airline.

- **Hotel-affiliated cards.** These cards offer points that can be used for flights or hotel stays—but the hotel stays are usually the much better deal. Typically, it takes about twice as much spending on a hotel card to earn a free flight than it would if you were using an airline-affiliated card. Hotel-affiliated cards might be a good idea for a traveler whose flights are usually paid for by an employer and who likes to add a day or two of sightseeing to the end of most trips.

You can research the various options at Web sites like CardRatings.com and Bankrate.com. If you're a frequent traveler, the Webflyer.com and FrequentFlier.com sites have terrific information about various airline- and hotel-related cards.

Match the card to your spending patterns. Both heavy and light spenders can run into trouble.

Cards that give you discounts on car purchases are among the most generous, but the rewards have their limits. The GM Card lets you earn 5% toward the purchase or lease of one of its vehicles, but the reward is capped at $1,000 if you want one of the company's more popular vehicles, like a Hummer or a Corvette. If you're willing to buy a minivan, though, you might be able to use a reward of up to $3,000.

The Subaru Platinum MasterCard from Chase gives you a 3% rebate on purchases but limits the total you can earn each year to $500. That means if you charge more than $16,667 a year, you won't earn any additional rebate.

If you want the discounts but you charge more than these levels, you can switch to another card (with a separate rebate program) after you've earned the maximum reward.

Light users face other problems. If you don't charge much, you can quickly pay more in annual fees than you'll get back in rewards.

For example, if you charge just $5,000 a year on a card that costs $60 annually, it will take you five years to earn a free airline ticket with most cards (assuming that one dollar spent earns one mile and that a ticket costs 25,000 miles). In that time, you'll have paid $300 in fees—enough to buy a discount coast-to-coast ticket on your own.

People who don't travel frequently with a specific airline often face frustration with trying to redeem their rewards. That's because the airline's elite frequent fliers usually get preferential treatment, leaving leisure travelers to face more restrictions and blackout days.

Even some of the no-fee, cash-back cards might not be the answer. Most don't give a full 1% back until you reach certain spending levels. Discover, for example, gives just .25% cash back on your first $1,500 of charges and .5% on the next $1,500, reaching the vaunted 1% level only on purchases above $3,000 a year. That means you'll earn just $7.50 on your first $3,000 in charges.

If you're a light user, you may be better off with one of the cards that offers 1% from your first purchase, such as the no-annual-fee Chase CashBuilder, or one that offers higher rebates for certain purchases, like cards that give you rebates for gas.

Understand the exchange rate. Frequent-flier miles are the gold standard of rewards. They're typically valued at 1 or 2 cents apiece. (However, they might be worth as much as 8 or 9 cents if you use them for upgrades on cheap coach tickets, says miles guru Randy Petersen of the WebFlyer online newsletter.) One or two cents is the same as a 1% to 2% rebate when you earn one mile per dollar spent.

Knowing the value helps in two ways. You'll know better than to choose a program that offers rewards of less than 1%. You'll also avoid squandering any miles you earn for merchandise or other conversions that give you much less value for your money—unless your reward is on the verge of expiring.

Know your limits. Speaking of expiring, you'll definitely want to know how long you have to use your rewards before they disappear. Some airline-affiliated credit cards have a use-it-or-lose-it policy, for example, as do many "travel reward" plans not affiliated with a specific carrier. (These programs let you book a flight on any airline, without blackout dates, but they usually limit the ticket's value to $500 or less.)

If you're not a big spender or won't be able to use your rewards for several years, make sure you have a card that allows you to bank your rewards. American Express and Diners Club, for example, are two cards with frequent-flier miles that don't expire.

If you can't use your miles to fly, you typically have plenty of other options. Most airline and travel reward cards give you alternatives, such as using your points to buy merchandise or hotel stays.

The conversion rate may not be great, though, which is why you want to use this only as a last resort. While 25,000 miles would buy you an airline ticket worth $500, for example, the same miles might pay for a hotel stay worth just $250 or merchandise valued at $100 or less.

You may also be able to convert your miles with one airline to another at a place like Points.com, but expect to lose 80% to 90% of their value in the conversion process—not a great option.

Protect your credit score. You may think you're being smart by charging as many purchases as possible to rack up frequent-flier miles or other rewards. But you could be damaging your credit score, which suffers when you use too much of your available credit limit.

It doesn't matter if you pay off your bill in full each month. As I explain in detail in my previous book, *Your Credit Score*, the credit-scoring formula typically doesn't differentiate between balances you pay off and those you carry month to month. What usually matters is the balance that shows on the statement the credit card company sends you each month, which it reports to the credit bureaus.

That's why it's smart to limit your charges to no more than 30% of your available limit. If you go over 30%, consider sending in a significant payment a week or more before your card's "statement closing date" (the last date that purchases and payments are recorded for the month). The closing date is usually listed on your statements; if not, call your issuer and ask. Reducing your balance owed in this way may help limit the ding on your credit score.

Summary

Credit cards can offer convenience, buyer protections, and even a source of emergency cash. But credit card *debt* is almost always toxic and should be among the first debts you pay off.

Credit Limits

- The best way to handle credit cards is to pay them off in full each month. If you can't swing that right now, at least pay significantly more than the minimum balance.

- Using more than 30% of the available limit on any card can hurt your credit score. "Maxing out" your cards can lead to higher interest rates and penalties.

- Credit card issuers have invented a number of ways to "ding" their customers even if they don't carry a balance. Read the disclosures your issuer sends you and consider some kind of automatic payment system so you're never late.

Shopping Tips

- If you're carrying a balance, look for a card with a low, fixed rate. Use a separate card for any new purchases, and pay it off in full each month. Better yet, use cash.

- Don't keep bouncing balances from card to card. Use low-rate offers to help you pay down your debt.

- If you don't carry a balance, consider a rewards card. The best one for you depends on your spending patterns and goals, so do your research.

4

Mortgages

Owning a home can be a good way to build wealth over time. Homeowners typically benefit from rising real estate prices, and many (although far from all) get tax breaks to help subsidize the cost.

But homeownership isn't right for everyone in all circumstances, and finding the right mortgage can be an incredibly tricky affair. You can easily find yourself paying too much for both your house and your loan. In the worst-case scenario, you could be setting yourself up for foreclosure and financial ruin.

Getting good, objective information on home buying and mortgages is tough, however. There are a lot of myths and outdated information. The people who tend to know the most about these transactions—real estate agents and lending professionals—usually have a financial stake in your decisions, which should make you at least somewhat skeptical about whether they have your best interests at heart.

Once you've got your mortgage, your decision-making isn't over. You'll probably be bombarded with offers to help you refinance or pay off the loan early. These solicitations can sound incredibly good, but at best they give you only part of the story, and in the long run they may hurt you financially.

This chapter should help you answer the following questions:

- Should I buy a house?

- How much house should I buy?

- What kind of mortgage should I get?

- How do I get a good mortgage deal?

- When and how should I refinance?

- When should I prepay a mortgage?

First we need to bust some of the myths that cloud people's thinking when it comes to home buying.

Myth #1: Real Estate Prices Always Rise

"Buy land," the adage goes. "They're not making any more of it." That's true as far as it goes, but housing markets can be a lot more volatile than the saying indicates.

Ask anyone who lived in Texas, Anchorage, or Boston in the late 1980s, or Southern California from the early to mid-1990s, when home prices in those areas plunged. London and Tokyo are among the international cities that have experienced housing price crashes.

Once house prices fall, they can take years to bounce back. Home values in Los Angeles dropped more than 20% on average and took a full decade to recover their former peaks. Hundreds of thousands of homeowners were "upside down," owing more on their mortgages than their homes were worth. Unfortunately, the economic recession that prompted the real estate crash also cost many homeowners their jobs. Unable to sell their homes for enough to pay off the mortgages, many simply turned in their keys to the bank and suffered foreclosures.

A spike in foreclosures can start feeding on itself. Lenders don't want the expense of maintaining and insuring these homes, so they slash the prices of foreclosed real estate to sell quickly, which brings down the value of neighboring houses. That wipes out the equity of other overextended borrowers, and now they too may be more likely to walk away from their loans— leading to more fire sales and further depressing values.

Everyone tends to get more cautious. People who can afford to buy homes put off the purchase, waiting for prices to stabilize. That reduces demand for homes and may push prices lower. Lenders and investors that buy mortgages tend to get more cautious in tumbling markets, as do real estate appraisers, which can make it harder to get deals done. (If you want to hear a home buyer howl, just show him or her a home appraisal that's less than what he or she's agreed to pay.) It can take years for this spiral to work itself out, let alone start to reverse.

Eventually, home prices do recover, but those who have to sell in the meantime can really get burned.

Myth #2: A House Is a Great Investment

Financial planners will tell you that you shouldn't think of a house the same way you think of other investments, like stocks, bonds, or mutual funds. Here's why:

Big emotions. A house is where you live, love your partner, raise your children. You'd be a strange bird indeed if you felt the same attachment to a stock as you did to the place you call home.

Big transaction costs. You can buy and sell securities with relative ease and at little expense. By contrast, you may need months to sell a home. The seller typically pays a 6% commission to the real estate agent who handles the sale, while moving costs and closing costs on a replacement home often add another 4% or so to the toll. That means 10% of the value of your home disappears each time you sell and move.

Big carrying costs. Your mutual fund will never require you to cough up $10,000 to buy it a new roof. The so-called "carrying costs" of homeownership are enormous. They include mortgage interest, insurance, taxes, maintenance, repairs, and improvements.

Many homeowners, however, forget to subtract these costs when they measure the financial gain they've experienced over the years.

If you bought a house for $35,000 in 1970 and sold it in 2000 for $200,000, for example, you may think you've earned a whopping gain. In reality, you've only outpaced inflation by about 1 percentage point a year, plus you may have paid out more than $100,000 along the way in repairs, maintenance, and improvements. (A study commissioned by the *Wall Street Journal* in 1998 found that the price of keeping a typical home up to current standards over a 30-year period is almost *four times* the home's purchase price.) Add to that sum the amount you shelled out over the years for mortgage interest, property taxes, and insurance.

Viewed one way, you actually lost financial ground.

Homeownership *does* help people build wealth, though, even when their home prices don't go through the roof.

Most mortgages require you to pay down your balance over time. That's a kind of "forced savings" that helps you build equity over the years, even if home prices rise only modestly (which they typically do, averaging 6% a year over the past 30 years, according to the National Association of Realtors).

Many also believe the act of becoming homeowners helps people become more responsible with their money and more interested in other ways they can build wealth. In other words, you might be more likely to invest in your 401(k) and buy other assets that increase in value over time, rather than blowing all your money on consumables like cars, clothes, and cuisine.

The proof is in the pudding. Table 4.1 shows the dramatic difference in wealth of homeowners versus renters in every income bracket.

Table 4.1   *Average Annual Net Worth of Owners Versus Renters*

Annual Income	Owners	Renters
$80,000 and up	$451,200	$87,400
$50,000 to $79,999	$194,610	$25,000
$30,000 to $49,999	$126,500	$10,600
$16,000 to $29,999	$112,600	$4,240
Under $16,000	$73,000	$500

Source: VIP Forum, Federal Reserve Bank's Survey of Consumer Finances, 2001

So, yes, a house *can* be a great investment. But it isn't a slam dunk.

Myth #3: Buying Is Always Better Than Renting

How many times have you heard someone say, "I had to buy a house because I was tired of throwing away money on rent?"

The reality is that you're not tossing cash out the window when you rent. You're buying freedom and flexibility, things you give up when you become a homeowner. Just hear what Alice had to say:

"I owned a home for five years and got rid of it when I realized the home owned me," she wrote. "Getting reliable people for maintenance and repairs was a major hassle. Scheduling maintenance and repairs meant staying home from work and waiting for people who sometimes didn't even show up. I am now an apartment dweller and figure the rent pays for all maintenance and peace of mind."

The benefits of renting go far beyond having a landlord to do the dirty work. If you lose your job, or the area starts to deteriorate, or you hate your neighbors, you can move pretty easily, compared to the costs and delays you'd face as a homeowner.

You may face rising rents. But homeowners face rising taxes and maintenance costs.

Renting is almost always the best option if you plan to be in an area for less than three years. Typically, it takes at least that long for home price appreciation to cover your selling and moving costs. It may take less in a super-hot market—or it may take much more if the bubble bursts and home prices fall.

Myth #4: Homeownership Comes with Great Tax Breaks

It's true that mortgage interest is *potentially* deductible on your tax return, as are the property taxes you pay. But many people overestimate the extent of those tax breaks and often misunderstand how they work.

Mark is an attorney in Frederick, Maryland, who shared many people's misconceptions about the potential tax benefits of homeownership.

"Homeowners get 100% of their interest payments back on their annual tax returns, right?" he wrote. "If I accumulate principal with each mortgage payment and get all of my interest back when filing my taxes, then it does compare favorably to renting, doesn't it?"

In reality, the amount of your tax break is limited to your tax bracket. If you're in the top federal tax bracket (35%), every dollar you pay in mortgage interest saves you at most 35 cents in federal income taxes. If you're a middle income taxpayer, your savings might be 25 or 15 cents per dollar spent.

That's why it's so absurd when people consider, or actually obtain, mortgages because they "need the tax break." Where else would you give someone a dollar just to get 15, 25, or 35 cents in return?

And that's the best-case scenario. In reality, the tax break you'll actually get will be much less—or even nonexistent.

Here's the reality:

- **About half the nation's homeowners get no tax benefit.** To get any tax break from a home, you have to have enough deductions to itemize. Two-thirds of the nation's taxpayers don't, so they take the standard deduction. Some of these people own their homes outright, but many don't pay enough mortgage interest and property taxes to be able to itemize.

- **The tax break is less than you think.** Even if you can itemize, the tax break you get from homeownership only equals the amount by which your write-offs exceed the standard deduction, as I explained in Chapter 2.

  For example, a single person in 2004 got a standard deduction of $4,850—even if he rented and had no other potentially deductible expenses. If he paid $6,000 in mortgage interest that year, the only advantage he would have over a renter who paid no mortgage interest is an extra $1,150 in deductions. In the 25% tax bracket, that $1,150 extra in deductible interest is worth just $287.50. So instead of saving 25% on his taxes, his actual tax break compared to the amount spent on mortgage interest is less than 5% ($1,150 divided by $6,000).

  Of course, he might pay much more in mortgage interest, and have other potentially deductible expenses that he's only able to write off because he has a mortgage. If he paid $2,000 in property taxes, for example, that would boost his "extra" deductions to $3,150 and boost his tax savings to $787.50. But that's still less than 10% of the $8,000 he spent.

  The fact that you'd get $4,850 in "free" deductions (or $9,700 for a married couple), whether or not you spent a dime in mortgage interest, significantly reduces the effective tax break for most homeowners.

- **The tax break tends to disappear.** Most mortgages are "front-loaded" so that you pay the most interest in the first year and a little less every year after that. The standard deduction, by contrast, increases every year to at least match the rate of inflation. (Attempts to eliminate the so-called "marriage penalty" led to a significant jump in the standard deduction for married people in 2004; in 2002, it was just $7,850.) The combination of the two trends means that many middle-class couples who get any benefit at all lose the tax break within the first 10 years.

And remember all those other house-related expenses I outlined earlier, such as insurance, maintenance, and repairs? Those are never deductible on a primary residence.

The Right Reasons to Buy

So if none of these myths are a good reason to buy a house, what is?

First and foremost, you have to *want* to be a homeowner. It doesn't matter what your parents think or your friends advise or your tax guy suggests. If you aren't ready, you aren't ready.

That was the case for Richard in Raleigh, who wrote me about an article I wrote for MSN on the home-buying myths.

"I am getting tremendous pressure from my tax advisor and other folks to purchase a home, but after reading your column, it is for all the wrong reasons," Richard wrote. "Clearly, I am not ready to purchase a home, and this article helped solidify my decision."

If you can answer yes to the following questions, buying a home can make sense:

I plan to stay put at least three years and probably more. In a typical market, it can take three to six years for a home to appreciate enough to offset the costs of selling and moving. If you're in a particularly hot market—one that might be ripe for a price drop—your desired time frame might be even longer, since it could take many years for prices to recover.

I'm psychologically prepared. Renting is like dating, home ownership is like marriage, and not everyone is cut out for wedded bliss. Even if you can unclog your own drains, you'll still occasionally have to call a plumber, as well as take responsibility for all the other chores your landlord handles now.

I have some extra savings. It's a rare first-time homeowner who isn't shocked by how much money she spends on repairs, maintenance, and decorating in the first years in her home (not to mention how much time you spend at Home Depot!). Those who drained their savings buying the house can find themselves going deeper and deeper into debt. You'd be much smarter to make sure that after the deal closes, you still have savings equal to at least two months' worth of mortgage payments, and preferably much more.

I manage my money pretty well. That "forced savings" aspect mentioned earlier works only if you can resist the temptation to drain your wealth with home equity loans and lines of credit. If you're carrying credit card debt now, and you're not quite sure what's happening to all the money you make, put off your house search and clean up your financial house first.

Otherwise, you'll wind up like some of the clients that Kevin, a financial planner, sees in his Atlanta practice.

"One of the most eye-opening aspects of starting my practice and having prospects and clients share their financial secrets with me is the horror I see when folks get caught in the perpetual cycle of trading equity in their home to pay off consumer debt," Kevin wrote. "When I see how so many folks are highly leveraged with home equity lines of credit or interest-only loans, I think to myself, 'They might as well be renting.'"

How Much House Should I Buy?

If you've decided you're ready, you still need to decide how much mortgage you're willing to take on.

Again, this is not a decision you should put in the hands of your lender, your real estate agent, your family, or your friends. Chances are good none of these folks know what you can really afford. Your lender or agent may know every detail of your current financial life, for example, but they probably don't know when you want to retire, how many children you want to have, or how much you like to travel—all factors that influence how much of a mortgage you should take on.

Meanwhile, your friends and family may be pushing you to take on a too-big mortgage, because *they* did and it worked out okay for them. But you may be smarter about finances or unwilling to give up as much as they did.

Also, the idea that it's okay to stretch to buy a home made sense 30 years ago, but it doesn't make sense today. Here's what's changed:

Lenders. Banks used to be a lot more cautious about who got loans and how much. Traditionally, lenders wouldn't offer you a loan if your total housing expenses—mortgage payment, homeowners insurance, and property taxes—exceeded 28% of your gross income. They usually didn't want to see your total obligations (your housing expenses, plus any other loans or debt payments) exceed 36% of your gross.

Today, most lenders have dramatically loosened their lending criteria. Mortgage brokers tell me they've seen lenders approve mortgages that ate up 50% or more of the borrower's income. So you can see that it's fairly easy to get saddled with a loan you can't really afford. Lenders know you'll do whatever it takes to make that payment, even if it means giving up all your other goals or sinking into debt.

Inflation. Prices soared in the 1970s and early 1980s—and so did wages. Those big jumps in income made mortgage payments feel substantially smaller every year, so even those who overdid their debt felt pretty comfortable within a few years. Today, you can't count on double-digit income boosts to bail you out.

Incomes. Inflation isn't the only factor affecting incomes that's changed. Thirty years ago, more families were supported by a single income—which means that if the breadwinner lost his or her job, the other spouse could go to work to help save the house. When you need both paychecks to cover the mortgage, there's no one in reserve to take up the slack, and a job loss can quickly lead to foreclosure.

Retirement. A far larger percentage of the workforce had traditional, defined-benefit pensions 30 years ago. That means they didn't have to put aside big chunks of their paychecks for 401(k)s and IRAs if they wanted to have a decent retirement. Chances are good that you don't have a traditional pension, so if you don't save, your retirement could be pretty grim.

So how much should you spend on a house? Many financial advisors recommend capping your housing costs at 25% of your gross (or total, pretax) income. That limit would give most families enough maneuvering room so that they can save for other goals without becoming overly indebted or "house poor."

Consider an even lower limit if

- **You want kids.** Children are wonderful, but they're also a drain on budgets. Bankruptcy expert Elizabeth Warren of Harvard University says just having kids is one of the leading predictors that a family will end up declaring bankruptcy. If you want to avoid that fate—and have the freedom for one parent to stay at home for a while—don't opt for an oversize mortgage.

- **You have expensive habits.** If you love to travel—or restore sports cars, or breed horses, or pursue any number of pricey hobbies—leave enough room in your budget to follow your passion. Most people are willing to cut back to afford the home they want, but if you're not, buy less house.

- **Your income's all over the map.** Most people have variable incomes because of overtime pay, bonuses, and commissions. But if yours really is unpredictable, you might want to base your home purchase on the minimum you expect to make each year.

You may be able to boost your limit higher if

- **You're debt-free.** The 25% cap assumes that you have at least some other debt: car loans, student loans, credit card balances. If that's not the case, you can probably stretch further.

- **You don't have to save much for retirement.** Government employees and public school teachers tend to have very good pensions that promise to replace 60% or more of their incomes in retirement. If you don't have to save a small fortune for your golden years, you can afford to throw more at a house.

- **You're on the fast track.** Some people have a pretty good shot at much higher incomes in just a few years. If you're currently a public defender and you're about to join a private practice, for example, you can expect your income to spike, so stretching a bit now might work out all right.

Once you've got a limit in mind, you still need to figure out how much house it will buy you.

Most mortgage calculators you find on the Internet still use the 28%-of-total-income figure. If you want to see how much mortgage you could afford under other scenarios, adjust your income by using the multipliers shown in Table 4.2.

Table 4.2   *Mortgage Multipliers*

Monthly Payment Limit	Multiplier
25%	0.9
28%	1
31%	1.11
33%	1.18

In other words, if you want to see how much mortgage you can get using a 25% limit, multiply your gross income by .9 and enter the result into the calculators as your income.

What Kind of Mortgage Should I Get?

This decision used to be a heck of a lot easier; before the 1980s, mortgages came in one basic flavor. The rates were fixed, you paid them back over 30 years, and then you held a mortgage-burning party where you triumphantly set fire to your loan paperwork.

Spiking interest rates in the 1980s brought adjustable-rate loans, where borrowers got low "teaser" rates in exchange for the possibility that their payments would change with interest rate swings.

Today, the variety of mortgages available is staggering. One of the more popular options is the hybrid loan, which combines features of both fixed and variable rates. Typically, the loan is fixed for the first three to seven years before becoming adjustable.

Also gaining popularity, particularly in expensive real estate markets, is the interest-only mortgage. As the name implies, these loans don't pay anything toward the principal for the first few years. You pay just the interest and hope that rising markets build your equity for you.

Then there's the option or "flexible payment" mortgage, which lets you pick and choose how much you pay each month. You can make a full payment or pay only the interest. You can skip a payment or make an extra payment toward the principal.

Each of these loans initially offers borrowers lower payments than they'd get with a 30-year loan—sometimes much lower. But all expose borrowers to the risk that their payments will raise, perhaps sharply, in the future.

At the other end of the scale are short-term, fixed-rate loans that help you pay down your principal faster. When interest rates plummeted at the beginning of this century, many borrowers refinanced into 15-year fixed-rate loans so that they could own their homes free and clear in half the time of a traditional mortgage.

So, how in the world do you decide what's right for you?

There's no one right answer. It all depends on your plans, the prevailing interest rates, and your tolerance for risk.

There's a lot to be said for the traditional 30-year mortgage. Your interest rate is fixed for the life of the loan, so you don't have to worry about rising payments. If rates drop, you can always refinance. Meanwhile, you're paying off a little principal with each payment, that "forced savings" that helps you build wealth over time. Payments are lower than for a loan with a 15-year term, which can give you more financial flexibility. If you want to pay more toward your principal, you can, but you're not locked into higher monthly payments.

All that flexibility and stability comes at a price, however. Interest rates and monthly payments on 30-year fixed-rate mortgages will be higher than with many of your other options.

That's why many mortgage experts say you should match your mortgage to the length of time you expect to be in your home. Someone who plans to move in five years, for example, would be advised to choose a five-year hybrid loan or even an interest-only loan where the rate is fixed for the first five years.

The thinking is that even if you stay a year or two longer than you expected, you'll still save money compared to what you would have spent with a fixed-rate loan.

Short-term adjustable-rate loans are a bigger gamble. You know the payment will go up because you're paying a low "teaser" rate for the first few months that will eventually adjust upward to the "regular" rate. What happens after that depends entirely on what's going on in the economy and with the Federal Reserve, which controls short-term interest rates. If the Fed decides it needs to battle inflation, it will raise rates rather abruptly. If the Fed is worried about an economic slowdown, it could lower rates just as fast.

Most adjustables come with built-in safeguards. Typically, the rate isn't allowed to rise more than 2 percentage points a year, or 6 percentage points over the life of the loan.

But that's still a pretty big potential rise. An increase from 5% to 11%, for example, would about double the monthly payment on your mortgage.

The risk on interest-only loans is even greater. While many interest-only loans offer fixed rates initially, they usually change to variable loans after a number of years. At some point, the loan also will require you to start making principal as well as interest payments.

This can lead to huge payment shock. Instead of paying principal over 30 years, you're typically paying principal over 20 years or less. Table 4.3 shows what you might see with an interest-only $500,000 loan where the principal payments are required starting with year 11.

Table 4.3   *Interest-Only Loan*

Years	Rate	Monthly Payment
1 to 10	3.875%	$1,615*
10 to 30	3.875%	$2,997**

*Interest only

**Includes amortization of the principal over 20 years

This example assumes the absolute best-case scenario: Interest rates stay exactly the same—and near record lows. Neither is likely.

Table 4.4 shows a more frightening example in which interest rates increase to the loan's caps over the years. The first five years have a fixed rate, the second five have a variable rate that starts at 6.875%, and the final decades have the highest rate allowed, plus principal payments starting in year 11.

Table 4.4   *Interest Rates Increase to the Loan's Caps*

Years	Rate	Monthly Payment
1 to 5	3.875%	$1,615*
6 to 8	6.875%	$2,864*
8 to 10	9.875%	$4,114*
10 to 30	9.875%	$4,783**

*Interest only

**Includes amortization of the principal over 20 years

Most likely, your experience with an interest-only loan, or any kind of hybrid or adjustable, would be somewhere between the extremes. But you should at least know how bad things might get before you make the choice.

You also should do your homework before taking out an option or flexible payment mortgage. These are so complicated that I won't even attempt to discuss their pros and cons here. Just know that the interest rate can change as often as monthly, and if you choose to make less than a full payment, these mortgages can actually get bigger over time. Also despite the lender's assurances about your payments being capped, these loans can "reset" after a certain number of years, and your payments can jump significantly.

When people get into trouble is when they choose an alternative mortgage because it's the only way they can purchase the home they want to buy. At some point, their payments will rise, and they may be forced to sell prematurely if they can't afford the increased cost.

When you're evaluating loans, take the following steps:

- **Do the math.** Make sure you calculate exactly how high your monthly payment can go if you opt for anything other than a fixed-rate loan. If you don't know how to do the math, look online for a mortgage amortization calculator or ask your mortgage broker or lender to help. Don't accept the loan officer's blandishments that a variable-rate loan will "never" reach its caps. Nobody can predict the future of interest rates, and people have been surprised before. Make sure you'll be able to swing the higher payments or be willing to sell your house if worse comes to worst.

- **Consider your need for financial flexibility.** If your income is quite variable or you expect heavy expenses like college tuition payments in a few years, be careful about taking on a loan with payments that could spike. Many people choose an adjustable or hybrid loan for the low initial payments, only to find themselves trapped when payments rise.

- **Evaluate your tolerance for risk.** You may be willing to literally "bet the house" that interest rates will stay stable or that your income will rise sufficiently to manage higher payments. But if that's not the case, there's nothing wrong with opting for the safety of a fixed-rate loan.

- **Don't expect to refinance your way out of trouble.** When interest rates were near their historic lows in 2004, I interviewed several homeowners about why they'd chosen variable rates when they had no plans to move. Many of them shrugged and said they would just refinance to a fixed-rate loan if rates went higher.

A look at historic interest rates would have given them pause. Rates on variable and fixed-rate loans tend to rise and fall at about the same time. If their variable-rate loan payments shoot up, chances are good that the payment on a fixed-rate loan would be even higher.

SHOULD YOU GAMBLE ON AN INTEREST-ONLY LOAN?

You may think interest-only loans are a relatively new innovation. You'd be right—and wrong.

Interest-only loans actually were quite popular in the 1920s, when investors wanted to minimize their mortgage payments and throw their extra money into the roaring stock market. The 1929 stock market crash and a steep rise in foreclosures took the shine off interest-only loans for most homeowners.

A few brokerage firms continued to make the loans, however, to their wealthy clients who already had plenty of real estate exposure in their portfolios and who didn't feel the need to build equity in their homes.

As housing prices started to soar in recent years, interest-only loans started gaining wider appeal. The trend was goosed along by mortgage professionals who were trying to keep the refinancing boom going after most people had already traded in their loans for new versions.

As the name implies, interest-only loans don't require you to repay any principal—at least not in the early years. The interest rate may be adjusted annually or be fixed for a period (usually five, seven, or 10 years) before becoming variable. The interest-only portion may end after the fixed period, or it may continue for a few more years before principal payments are required. As with other adjustable-rate mortgages, there are typically caps that determine how much your interest rate can rise each year and during the life of the loan.

What catches most borrowers' attention is how low the initial payments are compared to those of other loans (see Table 4.5).

Table 4.5   *Initial Loan Payments*

Mortgage	Rate	Payment
Interest-only	3.88%	$1,615
Five-year hybrid	3.75%	$2,316
30-year fixed	5.75%	$2,918

Lower payments mean you can qualify to buy a lot more house, which is why interest-only loans have become so popular in pricey markets where it's difficult to afford a home.

Ironically, though, people who are using them to stretch to buy a home are among the worst candidates for these kinds of loans. Payments can jump as soon as the rates become variable, and they can jump again—sharply—when principal payments become mandatory. If you could barely afford the home when the payments were low, you might be in foreclosure soon after the first adjustment.

Another group of buyers don't want to tie up their money in a mortgage; they'd rather invest it somewhere else for a better return. They're content to let rising real estate markets build their equity for them, and they see no need to pay down their equity.

This strategy can work well when home prices are rising, but it can leave the homeowner stranded—owing more on the home than it's worth—if the real estate market tanks.

It's also a dangerous strategy for the financially undisciplined. If you use your smaller payments as an excuse to spend more, you won't be building wealth over time. Many people need the forced-savings aspect of a regular mortgage; otherwise, they just wind up poorer in the long run.

How Do I Get a Good Mortgage Deal?

Figuring out which loan you want is just the start of the challenges you'll face. Finding and applying for a mortgage—and not getting soaked in the process—isn't easy.

You'll face stunning amounts of paperwork, fees that appear from nowhere, and a whole glossary of new terms to learn. It's easy for novices and even more-practiced homebuyers to stumble.

Fortunately, you have plenty of resources to help you through the process. Two of my favorites are *Mortgages for Dummies* and *Home Buying for Dummies*, both by Eric Tyson and Ray Brown.

Here are a few suggestions to help you navigate and get the best possible loan:

1. Fix your credit.

Pull your credit reports from all three bureaus at least three months—and preferably six months—before you apply for a mortgage. The information on your reports determines your all-important credit scores, and you'll want to have time to correct any significant errors.

Most people can improve their standing by paying down debt, paying all their bills on time, and not applying for credit they don't absolutely need in the months before they shop for a mortgage. (For more information about credit scores and combating credit report errors, see my book *Your Credit Score: How to Fix, Improve, and Protect the 3-Digit Number That Shapes Your Financial Future* [2004, Prentice Hall].)

2. Understand points and fees.

The interest rate is just one part of the mortgage puzzle. To shop effectively for a loan, it's also important to know what you'll be paying in points and fees.

A point is a percentage of the loan amount: One point equals 1%, or $2,000 on a $200,000 mortgage. People pay points to get a lower interest rate. One borrower might pay no points to get a 6% rate, for example, while another might pay one point to get a 5.75% rate. The longer you plan to be in your house, the more you might want to consider "buying down" your rate.

Fees are what lenders charge to process your loan. Lenders are supposed to provide you with a "good-faith estimate" of these charges within three days of your application, but many let you know up front what their closing costs are likely to be.

One particular fee you might want to ask about is the cost to "lock in" a rate. If rates rise between the time you apply and the time the loan closes, a lock can ensure that you get the original rate. But you should know how much this guarantee costs and how long it lasts.

Don't believe anyone who tries to sell you a "no-cost" mortgage. Loans almost always have costs, although they can be disguised as a higher rate or as fees that are added to your principal.

3. Shop around for rates and terms.

Thousands of lenders are out there, competing for your business. Don't just assume you'll get the best deal from the first one you call.

Once you know your credit score, you can find out what kinds of rates you can expect (see Table 4.6). The Loan Savings Calculator at MyFico.com gives you an idea of prevailing rates for people with scores similar to yours.

Table 4.6 *Mortgage Rates by Credit Score for a 30-Year $150,000 Loan*

FICO Range	Interest Rate	Monthly Payment	Total Interest Paid
720–850	5.703%	$871	$163,519
700–719	5.827%	$883	$167,776
675–699	6.364%	$935	$186,501
620–674	7.511%	$1,050	$227,983
560–619	8.452%	$1,148	$263,378
500–559	9.234%	$1,232	$293,619

Source: MyFico.com and Informa Research

Too many people with good credit get stuck with loans meant for people with lousy credit. These "subprime" loans are often more profitable for the lenders and the brokers, so less ethical mortgage brokers may push them over loans that give you a better deal.

Many borrowers are also sideswiped by last-minute charges and fees they hadn't anticipated. That's why it's important to ask about points and fees upfront and to deal with reputable brokers and lenders who don't dish up unpleasant surprise charges to their customers.

If you're comfortable using the Internet, you can visit sites like ELoan and Lending Tree to get competitive offers from lenders. The nice thing about these sites is that fees are disclosed upfront, which makes shopping easier.

Otherwise, you can call various lenders or get a mortgage broker to help you do your shopping. Brokers typically have access to a wide variety of lenders and loan programs. (Brokers can be particularly helpful if you're wading into the mortgage pool for the first time or if you have unusual circumstances, like bad credit.) Get referrals from friends and make sure the broker is experienced and is a member of the National Association of Mortgage Brokers, which has ethical and education standards.

One note: You'll want to do your mortgage shopping in a concentrated period of time—preferably within two weeks. Lenders typically pull your credit reports and scores before making their offers, and all those inquiries could wind up hurting your score unless they come fairly close together. The FICO credit scoring model treats all mortgage-related inquiries made within a 45-day period as one inquiry.

4. Check out first-time home buyers' programs.

These programs are usually sponsored by state, county, or city governments and typically offer better interest rates and terms than most private lenders, said mortgage expert Diane St. James of ABC Mortgage Consulting.

Many state housing agencies, for example, offer loans with below-market interest rates as well as programs that lend or give you cash for a down payment. And you don't have to be poor to get help; in high-cost areas like Boston, a family of three could have a six-figure income and still qualify for the state's MassAdvantage program.

These programs have some hitches. If you sell within nine years of getting the loan from a state agency, a federal tax could take back up to 50% of any profit you make on the home. (For more information, contact the National Council of State Housing Agencies at www.ncsa.org.)

5. Get preapproved for a loan.

If you're buying a home (rather than refinancing), you'll want to get preapproved for a loan.

Many first-time borrowers think "prequalified" is the same as "preapproved," but it's not. Prequalification is a pretty informal process in which a lender gives you a ballpark idea of how much it might lend you based on what you tell it about your income, your debt, and how much cash you have on hand.

Preapproval, by contrast, is a much bigger commitment. You usually have to submit tax returns, pay stubs, and other proof of your financial situation. The lender verifies the information and checks your credit before making a written commitment to make the loan.

If your real estate market is at all competitive, you'll want to put yourself in the best position to have your bid accepted. That's why you need to be preapproved—you're showing that a lender has checked you out and committed to make the loan. That's a lot more attractive to a seller than a buyer whose lender might simply back out.

6. Don't pay junk fees.

If you ask many mortgage brokers or lenders, they'll tell you there's no such thing as a junk fee—that everything listed on the good-faith estimates they're required to give to loan applicants is a legitimate charge.

Legitimate or not, many of these charges are quite negotiable. Entries such as "document preparation," "administration," and "processing" are mostly pure profit and can be winnowed out. Also look for padding on third-party charges, like credit checks; these shouldn't cost the lender more than a few bucks, but some try to zap you with a $150 fee. Ask about any charge you don't understand, and try to negotiate any charges that seem excessive.

You'll want to do your negotiating up front. If the lender or broker won't play ball, take the written estimate to another shop, St. James recommends. This is a competitive industry, and the borrower should be in the driver's seat.

If you've picked your broker or lender well, the agreement you negotiate should be the same one you see at closing (the day you sign the loan documents and actually get your mortgage). Unfortunately, there are bad guys in this industry that spring new or inflated fees on borrowers at the last minute. You can try challenging junk fees at this point, but most likely you'll have to swallow your anger and agree to the fees if you want to get your loan.

That's why it's so important to get referrals and check out a lender or broker's reputation before you apply. Lending pros that want to be in business for the long haul treat their customers well. Those that don't tend to leave a trail of dissatisfied customers behind them.

7. Plan for closing costs.

At closing, you'll be expected to write a sizeable check for a number of costs, including things like attorney's fees, taxes, title insurance, prepaid homeowners insurance, points, and various other fees. These closing costs can be fairly substantial—typically 2% to 7% of the house's selling price.

Your good-faith estimate should give you an idea of how much cash you'll need in your checking account. *But make sure these costs don't clean you out.* Too many people deplete their savings to buy a house and then wind up in debt—or even unable to pay their mortgage—when the furnace conks out or some other inevitable expense pops up.

You should plan to have at least three months' worth of mortgage payments in cash after closing, preferably tucked away in a safe, liquid place like a savings account or money market fund.

When and How Should I Refinance?

Your first mortgage almost certainly won't be your last. The typical homeowner keeps a mortgage for less than seven years before moving or refinancing. That holding period can be considerably shorter when rates are dropping and homeowners rush to exchange their loans for something cheaper.

Knowing when you should refinance is getting tougher. The old rule of thumb was that interest rates had to drop a full 2 percentage points for a refinance to make sense for most people. But that was back when everybody had 30-year fixed mortgages and refinancing costs were high.

Today there are so many different kinds of mortgages and so much competition driving down costs that rules of thumb don't really work anymore. You really need to take a good look at your individual situation and what lenders are currently offering.

Here's how to know if you should refinance:

Figure out what you really want. Are you just trying to lower your monthly payments? Or would you like to pay off your home faster? Are you looking to get cash to pay for a home improvement or other project? Your goal will help determine the kind of loan and costs you'll face.

Sometimes you can accomplish more than one goal. When interest rates were dropping early in this century, for example, some people were able to get "cash-out" refinancings and still lower their monthly payments. But most of the time, you'll have to decide which goal is most important, and this will dictate the kind of loan you'll be shopping for.

Run the numbers. Use the earlier advice about shopping for a mortgage to get a clearer idea of how much refinancing will cost you, and then use one of the mortgage refinancing calculators available on the Web to crunch the numbers. (You can find a good one at www.hsh.com/usnrcalc.html.) This will show you your "break-even" point: when (or if) the savings from the new loan will offset the costs of refinancing.

If it's three years or less, and you're sure you'll be in the house that long, you can consider going ahead. Any mortgage refinance with a break-even point more than three years out is a risky proposition, since chances increase that you'll sell the house before you recoup the costs.

In fact, some mortgage experts say you should be cautious if the refinance will take more than 18 months to break even.

Here are some other signs that you're better off not refinancing:

- **You've been paying the loan for several years.** By the time you're 10 or 20 years into a 30-year loan, for example, much of your payment is going toward principal. Refinancing to another 30-year loan would probably just increase your costs in the long run.

- **Your credit has deteriorated significantly.** Have you missed payments, maxed out your credit cards, or suffered a serious hit to your credit report, such as a repossession, collection, or judgment? Worse yet, have you filed for bankruptcy? You may not be able to get a rate low enough to justify refinancing.

- **You've stripped all the equity out of your house.** To get the best rates, you'll need to keep your borrowing to less than 80% of the value of your home. The rates you'll pay start to skyrocket if all your mortgages (your first mortgage, plus any home equity loans or lines of credit) equal 90% or more of your home's value.

- **You're facing a substantial prepayment penalty.** Some mortgages punish you if you refinance within a certain period. You might not realize you agreed to a prepayment penalty when you got your loan—you'll need to check your paperwork.

David in Illinois missed out on some of the lowest rates in a generation because of just such a clause.

"When we tried to refinance, we found out there was a huge penalty to pay back more than 20% of the remaining balance in a 12-month period," David said. "Needless to say, we couldn't refinance because the penalty would have meant almost an additional $5,000."

There's one more issue to think about. If you keep replacing one 30-year mortgage with another, you're putting off the day when your payments will significantly build your equity. Instead of building wealth by paying down your debt, you're basically "renting money" from the bank.

Some financial pundits insist that's a smart move. They think everybody should stay in perpetual mortgage debt. Their reasoning is that mortgage loans are cheap money and that you can get better returns on your cash elsewhere.

I agree with that view—to a point. I think most people want to have their home paid off by the time they retire. When you're on a fixed income, having a paid-off house can give you enormous peace of mind. Not having a mortgage to pay also can reduce the amount of money you need to withdraw from retirement funds, which can help make your nest egg last longer (and usually lower your tax burden in the bargain).

That doesn't mean you shouldn't refinance if you're over 40—just consider a shorter loan. If you're five years into a 30-year mortgage, for example, think about refinancing to a 25-year loan. That way you can lower your monthly payments without extending your time in debt.

When Should I Prepay a Mortgage?

Zach in Lake Forest, Illinois, was intrigued by the offers he got in the mail to help him pay off his mortgage faster.

These services offer to help you set up a biweekly payment program to shave your loan costs. Rather than pay $1,199 a month on a $200,000 mortgage, for example, Zach would pay $599.50 every two weeks. Since there are 52 weeks in a year, he'd be making 26 half-payments—the equivalent of 13 full payments, or one more payment than he would otherwise make.

The biweekly plan, the service promised, would shave five years and $47,282 in interest off the cost of a 30-year mortgage, assuming it had a 6% interest rate.

"Is this any different from just prepaying that one extra payment per year?" Zach asked in an e-mail. "The reason I ask is there is a $400 enrollment fee [for the service], and it seems math-wise that I could do the same thing paying a few hundred dollars extra each month."

Zach's right—the effect of making 26 half-payments or 13 full payments is basically the same. If you opt to prepay your mortgage, you don't need to pay anyone to set up the system. You can either set the money aside throughout the year to make an extra payment, or add a bit to each mortgage payment to get your loan paid off faster. (Just make sure the lender knows the extra money is for principal repayment.)

Before Zach or anyone else sets up such a plan, he needs to take a good look at the state of his finances and make sure all his other bases are covered.

It makes no sense, as I said earlier, to prepay a low-rate mortgage when you've got high-rate debt accumulating interest elsewhere. Generally, a mortgage is the very last debt you'll want to pay off, tackled only after all your other bills—credit card debt, auto loans, student loans, whatever—have been retired.

You'll also want to make sure you're taking full advantage of your tax-deferred retirement options, like contributing the maximum to your company's 401(k)—particularly if it has a match. The returns you're likely to get in those plans far exceed the returns you'll get from paying off a mortgage.

You'll want to check to make sure your loan doesn't have prepayment penalties; unfortunately, some do.

Finally, you'll want to follow your mortgage lender's instructions to the letter about how to get extra payments applied to your principal. Some people have discovered, to their horror, that their extra money was applied to the next month's bill and didn't reduce their principal at all.

Summary

Homeownership can help build your wealth, but you can easily end up paying too much for your house and your mortgage.

Credit Limits

- Buy a home when it's right for you. Don't be persuaded by common myths about homeowning or be pressured into a purchase when you're not ready.

- Try to cap your housing costs at 25% of your gross income to give yourself some financial flexibility.

- Consider matching your mortgage type to the length of time you expect to be in the house. But don't automatically discount the traditional 30-year, fixed-rate mortgage, which offers stability and flexibility for many buyers.

Shopping Tips

- Refinance when it makes sense for your particular financial situation. There are no rules of thumb; the decision rests on your goals, your credit situation, how long you've been paying your current mortgage, and how long it will take to recoup your costs.

- Know all the costs that come with a mortgage—the interest rate, the points, the fees—and shop hard. Thousands of mortgage lenders out there are ready to compete for your business; don't assume you'll get the best deal from the first one you call.

- Don't pay someone to set up a prepayment plan for you. And accelerate mortgage payments only when the rest of your financial bases are covered.

5

Home Equity Borrowing

You don't want to squander your home equity—a long-term asset—on short-term spending. That's why I've written several articles for the MSN Money site warning consumers not to tap their equity to pay for stuff like vacations, big-screen TVs, and credit card debt.

Almost inevitably, the articles are accompanied by big ads from lenders urging consumers to tap their home equity to pay for stuff like vacations, big-screen TVs, and credit card debt.

Some readers see the irony and send me e-mails about the contrast between my sober admonitions and the "Borrow! Borrow! Borrow!" siren song of the ads.

But many people, I'm afraid, miss the advice altogether and just go for the loan.

The voices encouraging you to spend your home equity freely are, unfortunately, loud and numerous. If you own a home, your mailbox is probably filled with come-ons for low-rate home equity loans. Lenders' ads for home equity lending fill the airwaves, and even your tax pro may get into the act, urging you to consolidate your debt into a tax-deductible package.

There are cases where a home equity loan or line of credit can be a smart solution. But too often it's used to fuel unwise spending.

The Dangers of Home Equity Lending

Katy owned a nice house in a Los Angeles neighborhood where prices had been growing at a double-digit clip. But the rising value of her home wasn't making Katy wealthier. Instead, every year or so Katy would drain off her equity to pay credit card bills, replace her late-model car, or take a vacation. She thought she was being smart by taking on tax-deductible debt. Instead, she was blowing her most important asset with pretty frivolous spending.

Her borrowing got to the point where she had very little equity left. When she tried to refinance her home loans, she learned that lenders wanted to charge her much higher interest rates because her existing house debt already totaled nearly 100% of the value of her home. (You get the best rates on home equity lending if your total borrowing equals 70% or less of the value of your home; once you get to 90%, rates really spike.)

What's more, Katy had left herself very little maneuvering room in case of emergency. Many people have to fall back on borrowing their home equity when confronted with a financial disaster like a job loss, catastrophic illness, or divorce. Since Katy had already "consumed" her financial cushion, she would have been in a pickle if she'd needed to get her hands on money fast. (As a rule of thumb, you should try to keep an equity cushion of 20% or more in your home.)

Another risk she faced was losing her home. If money got tight and she missed enough payments, her home equity lender could foreclose on her house. When interest rates were low, that didn't seem like much of a possibility. As rates rose in 2005, though, she found herself having more trouble making her minimum payments.

Using up all your equity in a fast-rising real estate market poses another, more hidden danger. Hot markets can cool suddenly, and prices can drop—as they did in Los Angeles in the early 1990s. Homes on average lost 20% of their value; some plunged 40%. If Katy had to sell into a falling market, she could find herself owing more on the house than she could sell it for.

All the dangers of home equity borrowing haven't dampened homeowners' appetites for these loans, however—far from it.

Home equity lending has soared tremendously in recent years, as shown in Table 5.1. New borrowing grew by nearly four times in five short years, and the amount we owe on home equity loans and lines of credit, $719 billion, now exceeds the balances on our Visas, MasterCards, and other general-purpose credit cards.

Table 5.1 *Home Equity Lending Soars*

	2004	**1999**	**Increase**
New Borrowing	$431 billion	$114 billion	278%
Total Owed	$719 billion	$267 billion	169%

Source: SMR Research

These figures reflect only mainstream home equity lending and don't include loans to folks with bad credit. This "subprime" mortgage market has grown even faster and now totals more than half a trillion dollars.

Less than a third of all this borrowing, lenders say, is used for anything that could remotely be considered an investment, such as home improvements or education. The rest goes for debt consolidation, vacations, or purchases of assets that quickly depreciate, such as cars.

Before we get into good and bad uses of home equity, though, let's review some of the basics.

Home Equity Loans Versus Lines of Credit

With both types of home equity borrowing, you're pledging your house as collateral. Both also offer potentially tax-deductible interest (up to a loan amount of $100,000).

You need to be able to itemize to deduct the interest, and you could lose this deduction if you're subject to the Alternative Minimum Tax, a nasty parallel tax system that affected about four million taxpayers in 2004. (Under the AMT, only home equity borrowing that's used to fund home improvements is considered deductible.)

Another important point is that you shouldn't have to pay much, if anything, to get a home equity loan or line of credit. The lending business has become so competitive that most lenders waive appraisal fees and other origination costs. If you get a line of credit, you may have to withdraw a certain amount to get the free setup, and you may pay an annual fee to maintain the account. If you're not borrowing more than 70% to 80% of your home's equity, and your credit score is okay, you shouldn't face other costs.

Here's how home equity loans and lines of credit vary:

Home equity loans are installment loans, like regular mortgages and auto loans. You typically receive your loan proceeds all at once and are expected to pay back the money over five to 15 years (although sometimes the loan term is longer).

Your payments typically are fixed, as is your interest rate. The rates on home equity loans are usually 1 to 2 percentage points higher than on a 30-year fixed-rate mortgage, but they vary according to your credit score (see Table 5.2). People with mediocre to poor scores can pay rates that are 3 to 7 percentage points higher than a typical mortgage.

Table 5.2   *Home Equity Loan Rates by Credit Score for a 15-Year Fixed-Rate $50,000 Home Equity Loan*

FICO Range	Interest Rate	Monthly Payment	Total Interest Paid
720–850	7.761%	$471	$34,772
700–719	8.061%	$480	$36,326
675–699	8.561%	$494	$38,949
620–674	9.336%	$517	$43,092
560–619	10.836%	$563	$51,369
500–559	12.086%	$603	$58,514

Source: MyFico.com and Informa Research

A home equity loan is usually the right choice when you pretty much know the cost of your purchase or project and you need several years to pay it off. A major home-improvement project, for example, might be a good candidate for a home equity loan.

You also might consider a loan when you want to lock in a low interest rate in a rising-rate environment.

Home equity lines of credit are more like credit cards. You have a credit limit that you can borrow against, and paying down your debt frees up more credit that you can spend if you want. Home equity lines of credit (HELOCs) have variable interest rates that are typically tied to the prime rate. If your credit score is excellent—760 or above—and your total borrowing against your home doesn't exceed 70% of its value, you should expect to get a rate up to half a point below the prime. People with less-sterling scores can pay up to 5 points above prime. See Table 5.3.

Table 5.3   *Home Equity Lines of Credit Rates by Credit Score for a $50,000 Adjustable-Rate Line*

FICO Range	Interest Rate
720–850	6.791%
700–719	7.166%
675–699	8.416%
620–674	9.791%
560–619	11.291%
500–559	12.791%

Source: MyFico.com and Informa Research

A line of credit is often better for shorter-term borrowing, or when you may need to tap your equity for different amounts over time.

HELOCs differ from credit cards in that they're typically not open-ended. HELOCs usually allow you to borrow against your limit for the first 10 years or so and pay only the interest charges. After that, however, the "draw" period ends, and you're required to start paying principal and interest to pay off your debt.

You may be able to extend your draw period with some lenders or refinance to a new home equity line of credit that offers a new draw period.

The way most homeowners pay off their home equity debts, however, is when they sell their homes. The balance of what they owe is deducted from their sale proceeds. This can make home equity borrowing seem almost painless, since you're not writing check after check to retire the debt.

But remember, if you hadn't borrowed with a home equity loan or line of credit, you'd have that much more money to use to buy your next home or pay for whatever other long-term goal is most important to you.

For example, the wealth you build up in your home can help you afford a comfortable retirement. Many people near retirement discover they haven't saved enough to quit work, or their investments haven't performed as well as they hoped. But if these folks have substantial home equity, they can sell their houses, downsize to smaller places, and have piles of cash to live on.

Other people use their home equity to fund college educations or to add rooms as their families expand. Again, the money to pay for these dreams won't be available if it's already been spent on less important things along the way.

Questions to Ask Before You Borrow

Any time you're tempted to use your home equity, ask yourself how important the purchase is. Will it help you achieve one of the most significant goals in your life? Homes are most people's major source of wealth, and that wealth shouldn't be frittered away on anything that's not close to their hearts.

You also should think twice about spending home equity on anything that doesn't gain in value. Your equity, if left alone, will rise over time. You don't want to blow it on a bunch of purchases that will soon have little or no value.

That said, let's deal with some of the most common ways people spend their home equity.

Paying off credit card debt. It's so tempting to pay off high-rate, nondeductible credit card debt with low-rate, potentially-deductible home debt. But the unwary face all kinds of traps.

One of the biggest is that you'll just end up running up more debt because you haven't corrected the problem that led you to overspend in the first place.

Credit card debt is short-term debt, which generally should be paid off using your current income. Transferring it to a home equity loan or line of credit can turn it into long-term debt. If you don't pay it off quickly, you could actually wind up paying more in interest than if you'd buckled down and paid off the cards.

You're also replacing unsecured debt, which could be wiped out in bankruptcy court, with debt that's secured by your home. If your overspending leads you to go broke, you may well regret nailing yourself to this debt.

If you do decide to use home equity to pay off credit cards, make it a one-time event. Cut up your credit cards and learn to live on cash until you're sure you can live within your means.

Paying for vacations, weddings, and big-screen TVs. I've actually heard some lenders try to justify this kind of misspending, but it's a nonstarter. Luxuries should be paid for with cash, not credit, and certainly not using your most important asset. If you can't afford it without touching your equity, you can't afford it.

If you've already succumbed, make a pact with yourself to pay off the debt as quickly as possible.

Buying stocks, real estate, or other investments. I know one woman who used the equity in her first home, a duplex, to purchase an apartment building and then leveraged the equity in that to buy a single-family home. She did all this in the pricey San Francisco area, on a very modest salary. She took a calculated risk, and it paid off handsomely.

But leverage can work against you, too. That stock you're sure will sky-rocket could become worthless tomorrow; that apartment building might be taken over by a violent gang, or simply sit with too many vacant units. If the value of what you're buying could drop to zero—which is true of any stock and many other investments, although it's rarely true of real estate—don't use your home equity to buy it. In any case, before you pull out equity to invest, understand the risks you're taking and try to keep at least a 20% cushion of equity in your home in case things go wrong.

Buying cars. Cars and other vehicles lose value pretty fast, which doesn't make them particularly good candidates for your home equity. On the other hand, if you have to borrow to buy a vehicle anyway, you may be able to get a lower and potentially tax-deductible rate if you use your home, rather than the car, to secure the debt.

What you don't want to do is let this debt ride for a decade or more, paying only the minimum required. In general, the life of any loan shouldn't exceed the life of whatever you buy with the money, and that's particularly true here. A much better course is to pay back the loan within three or four years. That will free up your equity to be reused for other, better purposes and keep you from overspending on your vehicle.

Education. Now you're getting warmer. Getting your kid through State U. isn't a traditional investment in that it probably won't increase your personal net worth. But it's an investment in her future that should pay off abundantly during her lifetime. Most studies show that college educations pay for themselves by the time the graduate is in her early 30s, even when you take into account the income she missed by not working full-time during her college years.

Not every parent feels an obligation to help with college, of course, and kids can always get their own student loans. If you do want to help, you should also investigate PLUS loans, which allow you to borrow for a child's education without using your home as collateral. (You can find more information at the U.S. Department of Education's financial aid Web site, http://studentaid.ed.gov.)

If you opt for a home equity loan or line of credit, be sure to keep your borrowing reasonable. Don't let your total mortgage debt exceed 80% of the value of your home, and make sure you can afford the monthly payments. You don't want to wind up losing your house and having to move into your kid's dorm room.

Emergency funds. Plenty of financial planners recommend that their clients set up home equity lines of credit to tap in case of emergency. This is seen as a supplement to any cash savings their clients have accumulated.

Given how little savings most families have, this is probably a smart idea—if you have the discipline to leave the line of credit alone. Every dollar you spend on something frivolous is a dollar you won't have when you need it.

If you decide to go forward, this is definitely something you'll want to have in place *before* you lose your job. You might still be able to get the line of credit afterward, but you're likely to pay a higher rate for the privilege.

Home improvements and repairs. You may think this is a slam dunk. Doesn't fixing up your home add value? Isn't that the kind of appreciating asset that home equity is supposed to fund?

There are a few flaws in that thinking. The first is that *repairs* don't really add value; they just keep your home's value from sinking. The next buyer will expect that you kept your home in good shape. If you didn't, the repairs the buyer has to make usually are deducted from the offering price.

The best way to pay for repairs is with cash. Personal finance guru Eric Tyson recommends putting aside 1% of your home's value each year to pay for repairs. Some years you won't use all the money, but you'll make up for that in the years when you need a big fix, like a new roof or heating system.

If the furnace conks out before you can put the cash together, a home equity loan or line of credit may be your next-best recourse.

Now to home *improvements.* These usually add less value than you think, and that value tends to wane, not grow, over time (see the sidebar near the end of this chapter).

People also can delude themselves that they "need" to remodel. Home improvements are a "want," not a "need," that should be balanced with all your other discretionary spending. A remodeling project certainly shouldn't replace or infringe on the money you need to be putting aside for retirement or other long-term goals.

If you decide to use your equity to pay for a remodel, remember that the money you're spending isn't really cheap—it's your long-term wealth.

Also you should know that although home equity loans and lines of credit are probably the most popular way to pay for home remodels, they're not the only options. You might also consider the following:

Cash-out refinancing. You basically get a new, larger mortgage to replace your existing home loan and get extra cash to pay for improvements and repairs. This could be a good choice if

- Interest rates have dropped since you got your current mortgage.

- You'll be in the home long enough to recoup your refinancing costs.

- Your project adds lasting value to your home.

Title 1 loans. If you don't have enough equity in your property to fund needed improvements or repairs, you may be able to borrow up to $25,000 through the Federal Housing Administration's Title 1 program. The loans are offered through banks and other lenders, and the interest rates are negotiable. Your interest payments, though, typically aren't deductible, and the loan can't be used for luxuries, like adding swimming pools.

Construction loans. If you're looking at a major remodel, and you don't have enough equity to pay for it, consider a construction loan. They're typically offered by regional banks and mortgage companies, but you can also find them at some national lenders like Bank of America and Wells Fargo.

Construction loans are short-term, interest-only loans that are designed to be replaced by a regular mortgage once your remodel is finished. Lenders may base the amount you get on your projected costs of construction, the future value of your home, or both.

These loans differ from mortgages and home equity borrowing in that you don't get the money all at once. Lenders typically dole out your funds in five to 10 "draws" timed to various stages of construction.

Construction loans come in two types:

- **The all-in-one loan** (also called the rollover or construction-to-permanent loan) becomes a standard mortgage after construction is completed. The borrower pays only one set of fees, and there's only one closing, which reduces the hassles.

- **The construction-only loan** must be paid off or replaced by a conventional mortgage once construction is completed. That means more fees and hassles, but borrowers may be able to get better rates on the replacement mortgage.

In either case, interest rates on construction loans are usually fixed for the life of the loan, which is typically a year or less. If you have good credit, you may be able to swing a rate as low as prime, although most people have to pay an additional percentage point or two.

That may seem like an extremely low rate, given how risky construction projects can be. But the lender gets its pound of flesh. You'll also pay fees—lots of them, to cover everything from origination costs to the lender's inspections of the project's progress. It's not unusual for the lender's fees to total 10% to 15% of the construction's cost.

You'll probably want to shop around to get the best deal, getting quotes from at least three different banks and mortgage lenders that specialize in construction loans.

THE TRUTH ABOUT REMODELING

You've probably seen articles and charts that purport to show which remodeling projects are the best "investments" for your home.

Don't believe them.

Investments are supposed to turn a profit. But very few home projects actually add more value to your house than they cost. At best, you may get 50% to 75% of your money back—and that's if you sell within a year or two of completing the project. And who wants to sell right after they've survived remodeling hell?

The reality is that, far from appreciating over time, the value of most projects starts to decline as soon as the paint dries. The trendy kitchen becomes dated, the new fixtures age, the materials and colors you thought were timeless appeal to fewer and fewer buyers as time passes.

That doesn't mean you should ignore resale value, particularly if you're tapping your home's equity to pay for the project. Like a car that doesn't depreciate much, a home improvement project with some chance of a return is usually better than one that won't add much value in buyers' eyes or that actually could detract from the potential sale price.

With so much at stake, you need to be careful about what projects you pick and about keeping costs reasonable.

The best bets for remodeling projects are any improvements or additions that bring your home up to the average for your neighborhood, said appraiser Diana Jacob, past president of the National Association of Master Appraisers in San Antonio, Texas. If most of the homes in your neighborhood have master bedroom-and-bath suites, for example, adding one to your house can make sense. If everyone else has run-of-the-mill Kenmore and you put in upscale Viking appliances, though, don't expect to recoup much of your cost.

In fact, the bigger and nicer your home, the less likely further improvements will benefit your bottom line. Homes that are worth more than 120% of the neighborhood average typically don't benefit much from renovations, appraisers say.

Also beware of projects that could turn off potential buyers. Pools and spas are often problematic because many people see them as hazardous hassles. Anything that limits the number of potential buyers could limit your eventual sale price (although the longer you plan to live in the home and enjoy the improvement, the less you may care about this potential downside).

Don't forget, when you're considering remodeling projects, to think about improvements that increase your home's energy efficiency. These may not add much to your home's resale value, but more-efficient appliances, windows, and light fixtures and better insulation often pay for themselves within a few years.

Skip the major remodels if you're thinking of moving in a year or two and are primarily interested in boosting your sale price rather than your quality of life. The relatively inexpensive projects listed in Table 5.4 usually have a much better payoff, according to HomeGain's survey of 2,000 real estate agents nationwide.

Table 5.4 *Home-Improvement Projects*

Improvement	Typical Cost	Increase in Sale Price
Lighten and brighten*	$86–$110	$768–$935
Clean and declutter	$305–$339	$2,093–$2,378
Fix plumbing and electrical	$338–$381	$922–$1,208
Landscape and trim	$432–$506	$1,594–$1,839
Staging**	$812–$1,089	$2,275–$2,841
Kitchen and bath upgrades	$1,546–$2,120	$3,823–$4,885
Repair flooring	$1,531–$1,714	$2,267–$2,589
Paint exterior	$2,188–$2,381	$2,907–$3,233
Replace carpeting	$2,602–$2,765	$3,585–$3,900

*Includes washing windows, removing heavy window treatments, and adding lamps

**Includes arranging furniture and accessories to highlight desirable room features

Summary

Your home equity is one of your greatest sources of long-term wealth. You don't want to treat it lightly or blow it on short-term spending.

Credit Limits

- In general, you shouldn't use your home equity to buy anything that declines in value.

- If you decide to tap your home's equity, try to keep your total borrowing (your mortgage plus any home equity loans or lines of credit) to 80% of your home's value. That will help you get good rates and terms, as well as preserve an important financial cushion for emergencies.

- Make sure you can make more than minimum payments on any home equity loans or lines of credit. If you can't manage that, you can't afford whatever you're using the home equity to buy.

Shopping Tips

- The rate you get on home equity borrowing depends heavily on your credit score. Check out the free Loan Savings Calculator at MyFico.com to see what kinds of rates you should expect, given your score.

- Contact several different lenders to shop for the best rates and terms. As long as you do your shopping within a two-week period, all mortgage-related inquiries will be counted as one, which will greatly limit the impact on your credit score.

- Don't pay a fortune to get a home equity loan or line of credit. Many lenders will set these up for free, particularly if you keep your total lending below 80% of your home's value.

6

Student Loans

Americans are pretty well convinced about the value of a college education.

Three-quarters of those polled for The National Center for Public Policy and Higher Education believe a college education is more important today than it was 10 years ago. People know that low-skill jobs are disappearing rapidly thanks to advancing technology, changes in our economy, and increased outsourcing of jobs overseas. A college degree is no longer seen as a ladder up; it's a life raft in a stormy economic sea (see Table 6.1).

Table 6.1 *Average Salaries for Those with College Degrees*

Degree Attained	Average Annual Pay
None	$18,793
High school graduate	$26,795
Bachelor's degree	$50,623
Master's degree	$63,592
PhD	$85,675
Professional (law, medicine)	$101,375

Source: U.S. Census Bureau, 2002

College degrees are also a profitable investment for most people. The College Board estimates that college graduates earn on average 73% more than a high school graduate over a 40-year working career.

As college enrollments have climbed, however, so have college costs. According to the College Board, the average cost of four years at a public university in 2004 was more than $45,000. The tab at private four-year colleges is more than $110,000. Those costs are more than one-third higher than they were 10 years ago.

The nature of financial aid has changed as well. Whereas most aid in the 1980s was in the form of grants, by the mid-1990s the greatest portion of student aid came in the form of loans.

These changes have led to a rather stunning rise in the level of student indebtedness. The average college student graduated with $18,900 of debt in 2002, up 66% in just five years. Those attending graduate school borrow another $31,700 on top of their undergraduate loans, a 51% increase.

Most people take on these enormous burdens at a time when they have no income, little credit savvy, and no clear idea how much this money will cost to pay back. Few realize what a crushing burden this debt can be—and unlike most other unsecured debts, student loans can't be wiped out in bankruptcy court, meaning that people are saddled with it for life.

I wrote about Michelle from Indiana in my previous book, *Your Credit Score*. She graduated with $120,000 in student loan debt, but her job at a university pays just under $50,000. She was contemplating bankruptcy, not realizing that a 1998 change in the law made it virtually impossible to erase student loan debt.

Kim also is staring at a debt she doesn't think she can repay. She went to college late, after she'd had four children. Now she teaches at a public school near Sioux City, Iowa, where a beginning teacher makes about $27,000. But her student loan debt is a whopping $87,000, and the small payments she can make don't even cover the interest owed.

"How will I ever be able to pay back this loan, plus the loans that I am now taking out for my two oldest children?" Kim wonders. "I have two more children who will be entering college in the next four years. I would love to be able to pay back these loans, but once again, how?"

Charles is in a similar fix, with student loan debt that's growing because his income is too low to make the minimum payments.

"I was prematurely forced to leave school near the end of my doctoral program because of a divorce. I have a huge student loan that I have no hope of paying unless I win the lottery," Charles wrote. "I can't make the full student loan payments and am on an income-sensitive repayment program... My loan just keeps getting bigger and bigger. I have inquired in just about every way I can think of for some way to get relief from my loan. It seems there is none."

Other student debtors find they can make their payments but can't afford to do much else. They postpone important goals, like buying a home or saving for retirement, so that they can pay down their student loan debt.

But putting off these goals is an expensive choice. A 22-year-old who put $4,000 into a Roth IRA, for example, could watch that money grow to more than $125,000 by the time she's eligible for full Social Security benefits. If she put off that contribution by 10 years, it would grow to less than half that amount—about $59,000. (Both examples assume an 8% average annual return.)

Few students are told about these potential costs, though, and most find no difficulty in getting loans to pay for as much education as they want. In fact, many students tell me they had no clear idea how much they had borrowed until they got their first bill six months after graduation.

Students do face maximums on how much they can borrow under federal student loan programs, but private lenders have no such limits. They usually give students, or their parents, the difference between their college costs and any financial aid they get.

Lenders can be so generous because they know how hard it is these days to default. Collection agencies have excellent systems for tracking down student borrowers and getting them to pay. The federal government can, and does, seize tax refunds and garnish wages when student loans aren't repaid.

So What's the Good News?

The good news is that student loan debt is usually flexible, relatively cheap, and available to folks who may not have much, if any, credit history.

Now, your debt might not feel cheap to you—particularly if you consolidated when rates were high and then watched others lock in rates of 4% or less as loans got cheaper. But historically student loans have been among the least expensive unsecured debt you can find. The federal government helps make sure of this by offering student lenders subsidies to make these loans available.

What's more, student lenders typically offer a variety of ways to structure and pay off your debt. If you lose your job or otherwise can't pay, you can get a forbearance or deferral for up to three years. If your budget's tight, you can opt for income-sensitive or graduated repayment programs.

Most borrowers can take longer than the standard 10 years to pay back their loans if they want. If Michelle tried to pay back her $120,000 in loans in 10 years, she would face a whopping $1,215 monthly payment (assuming a 4% interest rate). If she consolidated and opted for a 30-year repayment plan, she could get her monthly minimum down to $573, or less than half the original amount.

Stretching out the term means you may pay more in interest—typically, a lot more. The 30-year payback period would boost Michelle's interest costs by about $60,000.

But lower minimums can help you manage your student loan debt and still have money left over to save for retirement or buy a home. Such investments should ultimately offer a much bigger return than paying off a 4% loan.

How Much Should I Borrow?

Since lenders see no reason to limit how much you borrow, it's up to you to apply the brakes.

If you're a student, your student loan payments once you graduate shouldn't exceed 10% of your expected monthly gross income. That means you'll probably need to limit your total borrowing to no more than two-thirds of your first year's salary.

If you're a parent considering borrowing money for your child's education, first make sure you're saving adequately for your own retirement and can cover your other bills. Remember, your student can always get his or her own loans, but no one will lend you money for your retirement.

How much you borrow depends on your goals and inclinations, but all your debts—including mortgage payments, credit cards, car loans, and education loans—shouldn't eat up more than 35% of your gross pay.

Figuring out how much you should borrow is a bit complicated. Students won't know until after they graduate what their interest rates will be, since most loans have variable rates that reset each July 1. Many parents pay their share using home equity borrowing with variable rates, which also can't be predicted in advance. To be conservative, you should figure on a rate of about 8%. (Most student loans are capped at 8.25% to 9%.)

At 8%, each $1,000 you borrow will cost you about $12 a month to repay, assuming a 10-year loan. If you're a student and you borrow $20,000, your monthly payment would be about $243.

That payment level should be manageable if you make about $30,000. Such a salary level should be pretty easy to achieve if you're an accounting or business major, where the typical starting salary is around $36,000.

The payments might be tougher to swing if you major in the liberal arts. English majors average about $28,000, while psychology majors earn an average of $26,000. At those pay levels, you're better off borrowing no more than about $18,000 over your college career.

You can check average starting salaries in your field by visiting the National Association of Colleges and Employers Web site at www.naceweb.org.

This rule of thumb is meant to be a guideline. You may opt to borrow more if, for example, you can reasonably expect your income to climb pretty steeply after graduation. (Lots of law school graduates, for example, start out in low-paying jobs before moving on to get the big bucks.)

You may want to be even more conservative if either of the following is true:

- **There's any chance you won't get your degree.** Your education won't be worth much in the job market unless you actually graduate.

- **You're going back to school in midlife.** It's harsh, but people over 40 often face a tough job market, and they have fewer working years over which to "amortize" the cost of any education loans.

Lori in Westfield, Indiana learned those realities a little too late. She went back to school in her 30s after earlier earning an associate's degree, but she dropped out before graduation. Her combined student loan debt has swelled to more than $100,000—but so far the best job she's found pays less than $33,000 a year.

"I've since learned an incomplete degree is the same as no degree," Lori said. Her problems paying her debt have led to a basement-level credit score, and she despairs of ever having enough money to buy her own home or save for retirement.

If you discover that the amount you should borrow is well below the amount you think you need to pay for school, it's time to consider some alternatives:

- **Go to a college that wants you.** A school that's actively trying to recruit you often will offer a much better financial aid package than one where you're fighting to get in.

- **Consider cheaper schools.** Lots of students attend a two-year school first and then transfer to a four-year institution. It's the four-year school's name that will be on your diploma, after all. Another option is public schools instead of private.

- **Go to work.** A part-time job during the school year, a full-time job in the summer, or alternating a semester of work with a semester of study can help reduce the amount of money you need to borrow.

FINDING FREE MONEY FOR COLLEGE

The best money for college is money you don't have to pay back. And that usually means federal, state, and institutional grants.

Scholarships are great, too, but they typically make up less than 2% of financial aid packages, while grants comprise nearly 40%. (Student loans provide the rest.)

But grants are largely based on need and usually are handed out on a first-come, first-served basis. That's why it's important to get in line early.

You need to fill out the Free Application for Federal Student Aid (FAFSA). It is available at high schools and college financial aid offices, at various places on the Internet, or by calling the U.S. Department of Education at 800-433-3243. The earliest you can submit your form for the next school year is January 1.

You'll want to file the form as soon after that as possible. Many colleges' student aid deadlines are in early to mid-February, and they may run out of grant money before they stop taking applications.

Many colleges require other forms or information when handing out their own grants. This money is typically meant to round out student aid packages when federal and state aid is insufficient—or when the school is trying to recruit a desired candidate (yet another reason to go with a school that wants you). For details, check with the schools where you'll be applying.

State grants may require still another form. Most states have some kind of free-money program—again, often based on need, although some programs are also targeted to encourage study in certain areas, such as teaching or nursing. State student aid offices have details.

You also can check around for scholarships, but be aware that the idea that millions of dollars are lying around in easy-to-get but unclaimed scholarships is largely a myth.

Most of the unclaimed money is so highly targeted that your chances of qualifying are remote. And many other scholarships are intensely competitive. The 250 sponsored by Coca-Cola, for example, regularly attract more than 100,000 applications.

Finally, scholarship money you get on your own is often *deducted* from a college's financial aid package—and often it's deducted from the grants you would otherwise get, not the loans.

That doesn't mean you shouldn't try for scholarships, particularly if

- Your family won't get much financial aid.
- The aid you'll get will be loans rather than grants.
- Your college's aid package will meet only part of your need (an increasingly common occurrence).
- Applying doesn't take a lot of effort.
- Applying does take a lot of effort, but landing the scholarship would be a real coup for your resume.

You need to start your scholarship search before your senior year. You don't need to pay for advice or help; there are several free Internet search engines, including ones run by FastWeb, FinancialAid.com, and student lender Sallie Mae.

You can look offline as well, using books that summarize available scholarships, such as *Chronicle Financial Aid Guide*.

And don't forget your own community. Here's a list of places to check:

- **High school clubs, teams, and guidance counselors.** Ask the club's adviser, the team's coach, or your child's counselor to help you look for appropriate scholarships.

- **Employers.** Many large companies, and even some smaller ones, have scholarship programs for the children of their workers or the workers themselves. Ask the human resources department.

- **Unions.** Ditto for your local or national organization.

- **Religious organizations.** Check with your church, temple, or mosque.

- **Community service organizations.** The Rotary or Elks may offer scholarships for members and nonmembers.

- **Professional organizations.** Most fields have at least one professional organization, and these groups often have scholarships for members, members' children, or others who are interested in pursuing a career in that field.

- **Ethnic organizations.** You may know that the United Negro College Fund has scholarships for African-Americans ("A Mind Is a Terrible Thing to Waste"), but so do groups for those of Italian, Polish, Swiss, Chinese, and Armenian backgrounds, to name just a few.

- **City, county, or state government.** Georgia, for example, offers free tuition at in-state public colleges for those who maintained a B average in school.

Where Should I Get My Loans?

Student loans come in two basic types: those provided or sponsored by the federal government and those that are not. Federal loans usually offer better rates and terms than private education loans, which is why you should opt for those first.

(By the way, just because a loan is *sponsored* by the federal government doesn't mean Uncle Sam will be your actual lender. Private lenders like Citibank offer federal loans as well as private loans.)

Federal loans may be subsidized or unsubsidized. If they're subsidized, the government pays the interest while you're in school. Otherwise, the interest starts accruing from the day you get the loan, even though payments probably won't be due until you graduate.

Once again, you'll want to take maximum advantage of any subsidized federal loan programs before you opt for other loans. These need-based loans will be part of your financial aid package if you qualify. Subsidized loans include the following:

- **Perkins loans.** These come with a 5% fixed interest rate, and you can borrow up to a maximum of $20,000. Perkins loans can be canceled if you work in certain fields, such as nursing, law enforcement, Peace Corps volunteering, or teaching in a low-income area.

- **Subsidized Stafford loans.** Stafford loans have a variable interest rate that's capped at 8.25% and a 4% upfront fee, which is usually deducted from your payout.

If you don't qualify for a subsidized Stafford loan, you may be offered the unsubsidized version. You can borrow a maximum of $23,000 total for both subsidized and unsubsidized Stafford loans while you're an undergraduate.

If you're a student paying for college yourself, these unsubsidized loans may still be a good deal compared to what you could get from private loan programs. If you're a parent or have access to alternative funding—such as a home-equity loan that you can lock in at a lower rate—you might choose that instead.

One other major federal student loan program is PLUS loans for parents. (PLUS stands for Parent Loans for Undergraduate Students.) This program allows parents who have good credit to borrow the difference between the student's financial aid package and the full cost of his or her education, including books, supplies, room and board, and other living expenses.

Some loans, like Perkins loans, are made directly by the school. With others, you need to apply to a bank, savings and loan, or credit union that provides money under federal student loan programs. Your college's financial aid office may have a list of recommended lenders, but typically you can choose whichever lender you want.

Once you've exhausted your federal student loan options, you can explore private loans sponsored by not-for-profit organizations or provided directly by banks. The interest rates are usually somewhat higher, as are the fees, and your ability to land the loans depends on your credit history (which typically isn't a factor with federal student loans).

The four main private loan programs for undergraduates include Sallie Mae's Signature Loans, Nellie Mae's EXCEL Loans, Wells Fargo's PLATO Higher Education Loans, and The Education Resources Institute's TERI Loans.

What if It's Already Too Late?

If you've already graduated with a pile of debt, don't despair. You may have more options than you think.

Explore loan forgiveness. A variety of state, federal, and private programs either erase student indebtedness or offer subsides to help pay it off. Typically, you need to volunteer, perform military service, or teach or practice medicine in underserved areas.

Those who serve in the Army National Guard, for example, can receive up to $10,000 to pay off their education debts, while service in the regular Armed Forces can lead to cancellation of up to 50% of your federal Perkins and Stafford loans. Full-time teachers in low-income areas or who teach in fields like math or science where there's a teacher shortage can qualify for cancellation of some of their federal loans.

FinancialAid.com has a section on loan forgiveness that lists many of the available options.

Consolidate your debts. Consolidation allows you to refinance your student loans into one large loan with one monthly payment. You typically can choose a longer payback period than the standard 10-year term, and you probably should. Opting for a 20- or even 30-year schedule will keep your minimum monthly payment low, but you can always make bigger payments to get the debt paid off faster. This approach will give you flexibility in good times as well as bad.

Traditionally, consolidation also meant locking in an interest rate— something that benefited millions of borrowers when rates dropped to a historic low in 2004. (Some borrowers were able to lock in rates of 2% and even less.) The fixed-rate approach is under attack, however, since the federal government must make greater subsidies to student lenders when rates fall so low. Future consolidation loans may well come with variable rates.

You can consolidate with your current lenders or with just about any other lender that specializes in federal student loans. If you're unsure who your lender is, you can use the lender locator at the National Student Clearinghouse (www.studentclearinghouse.org) to find out.

Be sure to shop around before you choose. Most consolidators will knock a full percentage point off your interest rate after you make 36 on-time monthly payments, and many give you another .25% break if you agree to automatic electronic payments.

What if you've already consolidated? Many borrowers who consolidated when rates were near their peaks have despaired to learn that consolidation is usually a one-time deal: Once you've consolidated a loan, you can't do it again, even if interest rates drop.

At least one student lender, FinancialAid.com, has come up with a program that allows an already-consolidated loan to be refinanced to a *variable-rate* loan. FinancialAid.com's RightRate program promises you'll never pay more than you do now, and you can benefit if rates decline.

Consider alternatives if money is really tight. You can defer payments on your loans for a total of three years in most cases. Many lenders also offer "income-sensitive" or "interest-only" payment plans.

These are not the best option if you can pay the minimum you owe, since interest typically continues to accrue and swell the size of your loans. But if you're unemployed, underemployed, or otherwise facing a serious income shortage, these options can offer temporary respite.

What you don't want to do is ignore your loans or your lenders. Late or inadequate payments typically are reported to the credit bureaus, which will damage your credit score and ability to get future loans.

Defaulting—failing to make the agreed-upon payments for nine months or more—is even more serious:

- Your wages and IRS refunds could be seized.

- You could be sued.

- You could be held responsible for paying any collection costs.

- You'll be ineligible for other federal loans, such as FHA or VA mortgages, or additional financial aid.

- You can lose many of your repayment options, such as the income-sensitive approach.

If you've already defaulted, try to get back on track as soon as possible. Your lender may be able to offer you the ability to "rehabilitate" your loan. This means that in exchange for making 12 or so on-time payments, any mention of your default is erased from credit bureau records. (If your lender doesn't offer this option, the U.S. Department of Education does; you can contact them at 800-621-3115.)

What About Paying Off My Student Loans with Home Equity Debt—or Credit Cards?

Several people who consolidated when interest rates were high have e-mailed me with schemes to reduce their rate, and many hit on the idea of paying off their loans with home equity debt.

Others proposed different alternatives. One reader noted that her credit card was offering a 4.99% rate "for the life of the balance" and wondered if that would be a good way to get her lending costs down.

There are situations when trading student loan debt for other kinds of debt can be advantageous, but this kind of refinancing is fraught with peril.

Few debts are as flexible as student loans. If you lose your job, you can get a deferral or forbearance so that you don't have to make payments for up to three years. Try that with a home equity debt or credit cards, and you'll wind up in foreclosure or collections.

Up to $2,500 of interest on student loan debt is tax-deductible, and you don't need to itemize to get the break. (There are income limits; the deduction begins to phase out at an adjusted gross income of $50,000 for singles and $100,000 for married people.) As I mentioned in the preceding chapter, you have to itemize to be able to deduct interest on home equity debt. And credit card interest isn't deductible at all.

Credit card companies are notoriously fickle, besides. They can promise you one rate and, with just 15 days' notice, decide to renege. Any errors on your part—say, paying late on that or any other card—can result in a huge jump in your rate.

If you opt for a home equity line of credit, rather than a loan, your rate can climb as well, not because of any fault of your own but thanks to changes in short-term interest rates. Caps on HELOCs typically are around 18%, which is much higher than the 8.25% to 9% cap on your student loans.

Given all this, most people are better off sticking with their student loans and simply paying them down faster if they want to reduce total interest costs.

WHY COLLEGE COSTS SO MUCH

How did the price tag for a college education get so high? You can blame a combination of factors:

Capital spending. The nation's top schools have been competing to provide the best facilities, faculty, and even sports teams (to keep wealthy alumni donors happy). Cornell economist Ronald G. Ehrenberg, in his book *Tuition Rising*, describes this as a kind of "arms race" that helps explain expanding budgets.

The competition goes beyond well-endowed Ivy League schools. Other universities hope to boost their rankings with college-rating programs by spending on high-speed Internet access, new gyms, concert halls, and better student housing.

Faculty. Half to two-thirds of the typical college's budget pays instructional salaries. The median salary for a tenured professor is $76,200, according to the American Association of University Professors.

Blaming high tuition prices solely on professor salaries doesn't really make sense because most schools keep a lid on costs by using nontenured staff, including graduate students, instructors, and lecturers. Today 60% or less of the typical college's staff is tenured or tenure-track.

Productivity. Inflation in the nonacademic world is often tamed by increases in worker productivity. Better technology, improved equipment, and greater experience help workers work faster and better, which allows businesses to create more products for the same cost.

Colleges aren't in the business of making widgets. If you try to improve professorial productivity by increasing class sizes or class loads, the best instructors leave, and the college's reputation suffers with the all-important ranking services.

If anything, there's pressure to be less productive. Many colleges are trying to shrink class sizes and reduce class loads so professors can do more research and that way bring more glory to the college.

Financial aid. Most people don't pay the full sticker price for college. Financial aid lessens the out-of-pocket costs for the majority. (Loans just delay the pain, but most students and their parents don't factor in a loan's ultimate cost when deciding where to attend.)

When people don't feel the real cost of what they're buying, they tend to spend more than if every dollar increase came directly out of their wallet. That's why we spend more when we use plastic, and it's one of the reasons why the costs of our health-care system are spiraling out of control.

Here's how it might work. Top-Flight University announces a 10% increase in tuition. If TFU's old tuition was already busting your budget, and you were paying your own way, you might decide to transfer to High-Ranked State to finish your schooling. If enough others made the same decision, that would put pressure on TFU to reverse its decision or at least slow the rate of its increases.

In the real world, though, TFU just needs to boost its financial aid packages by 8% or so. The impact is muted, and the price increase stands.

The government has helped create this situation, too. Popular tax breaks like the Hope Credit and the Lifetime Learning Credit, student loan interest deductions, and tax-advantaged savings plans like Coverdells and 529 college savings plans help many parents soften the impact of rising prices.

I'm not advocating cutbacks to financial aid or tax breaks. But since higher prices don't result in a decrease in demand, there's nothing to put a brake on tuition hikes.

More applicants. Demographics explain a lot. They always do.

The number of college-age people actually declined for the two decades ending in 1997. But the proportion of this shrinking group that attended college shot up from 47% of high school graduates in 1973 to 65% in 1996. That meant the number of people attending college in the 1990s remained pretty stable.

Now the under-25 set is again on the rise. The number of college-age people is expected to grow from 17.5 million in 1997 to 21.2 million by 2010. The proportion attending college is expected to increase even more because of the trends I noted at the beginning of this chapter. Everybody knows that fewer and fewer good jobs are available to those with just a high school education.

The most selective schools haven't expanded anywhere near enough to meet the soaring demand. That's why the SAT scores that would have gotten you into the Ivy League in the 1980s might not get you accepted at a competitive state university today.

Other schools are trying to grow, but they often are hampered by inadequate legislative appropriations (if they're state schools) or lagging endowments (if they're private). So good colleges continue to have far more qualified applicants than they have slots available to educate them.

With that kind of demand, colleges and universities can continue to boost prices almost at will.

Summary

Student loans can be an investment in your future, but it's easy to overdose on this so-called "good" debt.

Credit Limits

- If you're a student, you should limit your total borrowing to no more than two-thirds of your first year's salary.

- If you're a parent considering borrowing money for your child's education, make sure you're saving adequately for your retirement before you commit to student loans. Your student can always get his or her own loans, but no one will lend you money for your retirement.

- Keep tabs on how much you're borrowing, the type of loan, and who you're borrowing from. It's easy to lose track of your total debt when you're borrowing from different lenders over time, as many students do.

Shopping Tips

- Federal student loans offer the best rates and terms, so take full advantage before you opt for private loans.

- For maximum flexibility, consolidate your loans and opt for the longest available payback period. You can always make larger payments to reduce your total interest costs, but most people find they have more important financial priorities than accelerating payments on their student loan debt.

- Most consolidators will knock a full percentage point off your interest rate after you make 36 on-time monthly payments, and many give you another .25% break if you agree to automatic electronic payments.

7

Auto Loans

Okay, I'll admit it. I don't get the car thing.

That's abundantly clear from the vehicles I've owned in my life, starting with the bright blue Mazda station wagon I purchased in college, followed by the Suzuki Samurai I drove in Alaska and the ever-thrifty little Saturn SL1 I bought with cash after arriving in Southern California. (I was so cheap at the time I refused to spring for electric locks.)

The few miles I drive now get added to the 240,000 or so already on the odometer of my SUV, a hand-me-down from my husband, who *does* care about cars—at least more than I do.

A friend explained that the difference between hubby and me is that he was *born* in California, where part of the natives' birthright is understanding that a nice set of wheels helps define who you are. As an import to the Golden State, I never got that information wired into my DNA.

If you too care passionately about what you drive, I won't try to talk you out of your love affair. That would be futile. At best, I'm hoping to moderate your ardor enough so that your vehicle expenditures don't wreck your overall financial plan.

If you're somewhere in between—you want a nice ride, but you hate the high costs and fear getting stuck with a lemon—I think you'll find plenty of information in this chapter that can improve how you buy, own, and pay for your vehicles. I hope to save you bucketfuls of money as well.

How Cars Cost Us

Transportation is a big part of the average American family's budget. The costs of purchasing, fueling, insuring, maintaining, and repairing vehicles are the second-largest expenditure on average, right behind housing (see Table 7.1).

Table 7.1 *Average Household Expenditures*

Category	Amount Spent	Percent of Total Spending	Percent of Pretax Income
Housing	$13,432	33%	26%
Transportation	$7,781	19%	15%
Food	$5,340	13%	10%
Other	$4,094	10%	8%
Insurance and pensions	$4,055	10%	8%
Health care	$2,416	6%	5%
Entertainment	$2,060	5%	4%
Apparel and services	$1,640	4%	3%
Totals	$40,818	100%	79%

Source: Bureau of Labor Statistics, 2003

The biggest chunk of our transportation costs (more than 70% of the total, on average) is the money we shell out to actually buy or lease the car. Unfortunately, many Americans are going about these purchases all wrong:

- They're driving into dealerships to buy new cars when they still owe money on their old ones. A stunning 40% of new-car buyers still have loans on their trade-ins, according to Edmunds.com; the average amount of negative equity is $2,220.

- They're stretching too far to buy the cars they want; 84% of all new-car loans are now for terms in excess of four years. With such long loan terms, it can take years for the driver to hit the break-even point, where he or she finally owes less on the car than it's worth.

- Gluts of used cars and incentives on new cars can make the problem worse by pushing down the value of older cars. That means as soon as you drive off the lot, your new car's value takes a big tumble—which can make it harder than ever to reach that break-even point.

Why It's Bad to Owe More on Your Car Than It's Worth

First of all, being "upside down" puts you at serious financial risk. If your car is stolen or totaled, you could find yourself without wheels and still owing thousands to your lender. (The amount you'll get from your insurer reflects the car's current, depreciated value—not what you paid for it.)

If you lose your job, you'll face a similar crunch. You might not be able to make your payments, but you won't be able to sell your car for enough to pay off the loan.

There *is* a type of specialized insurance, called guaranteed auto protection, that can cover the gap if your car is stolen or totaled, and you can buy credit unemployment insurance to make your payments if you lose your job. If you're underwater on a car loan, you should seriously consider these coverages.

But owing more money on a car than it is worth is a symptom of a deeper problem: overspending.

People who stretch too far to buy a car cost themselves in numerous ways. The first is in interest costs: The more you borrow and the longer you take to pay back a loan, the more you pay in interest.

Lenders typically charge a higher rate for longer-term loans. So while you might be able to swing a 4% rate on a three-year loan, you may pay 6% on a six-year loan.

Your payments on the longer-term loan will be lower: $331 compared to $590 for the three-year loan. But you'll have twice as many payments to make on the six-year loan, and your total interest costs will be $3,865—three times the $1,257 you'd pay with the three-year loan.

Then there are all the other costs associated with buying a new car. Your insurance costs typically jump; the more expensive the car, the higher the premiums. Repairs on newer cars can be costly as well, thanks to more-sophisticated technology. (If you've ever had to replace one of those high-intensity headlights, you'll find that they can be 10 times costlier than a halo-gen headlight and infinitely costlier than the old-fashioned lamps, which cost just a few bucks.)

As one Edmunds.com executive put it, many people discover they can afford their car but, thanks to all the attendant costs, can no longer afford to eat.

The more money you spend on your ride, the less money you have for other things in your life, including vacations, emergency savings, and retirement funds. Your choices are to cut back on your other spending, neg-lect your important long-term goals, or go deeper into debt trying to maintain your lifestyle.

SAVE ON CAR INSURANCE

Most advice on car insurance focuses on what you can do after you've purchased the car to lower your premiums—such as increasing your deductible, seeking out good-driver dis-counts, and using the same insurer for your auto and home.

But the real savings depend on a decision that comes much earlier: when you choose what car to buy.

Some cars are simply better built, cheaper to repair, and less likely to be in accidents in the first place because the drivers they attract tend to be safer. Insurers scour their claims data to discover which cars these are and reward their owners with better rates.

For example, I was astonished to discover from a recent Edmunds.com survey that a $14,000 Dodge Neon costs about the same to insure as a $34,000 Volvo XC70. Five years of insurance premiums on the Neon averaged $4,410, compared to $4,605 for the Volvo.

In general, you would expect a more expensive car to have higher insurance premiums. The costlier the car, in general, the more expensive the labor and parts to fix it, and the more likely it is to be stolen—all important considerations when insurance companies figure out what to charge.

But Volvos have a reputation for being "safe" cars; they protect their occupants better than the average car, and that reduces insurers' exposure to medical costs. Volvos also tend to attract older, more cautious, safety-conscious drivers; that's known as a "demographic," and it compares favorably to the less-experienced, more-likely-to-crash young drivers who tend to buy Neons. The Volvo also isn't as likely to be stolen, and it inflicts less damage than average on other cars when it is involved in a crash.

How do you find out how insurers view your vehicle? Edmunds.com's True Cost to Own feature can give you a pretty good guesstimate of how much different cars cost to insure. You also can check out State Farm's car ratings, which are listed on its Web site (www.statefarm.com). State Farm uses a system that grades vehicles on three crucial areas:

- Liability: how much damage the car causes to others in a crash
- Safety: how well the car protects its occupants
- Damage and theft: how likely the car is to be damaged, how much the repairs tend to cost, and how likely it is to be stolen

State Farm uses letter grades—A, B, and C—to assess liability, safety, damage, and theft. An A means the car performs better than average and qualifies for a premium discount. A B means it's average, so no discount is given. A C means the car performs worse than average, so the owner pays a higher-than-average premium. Meanwhile, the discount for safety ranges from 0% (no price break) to 40%.

The best way to use the ratings, according to State Farm spokesman Dick Luedke, is to compare similarly-priced cars. A Cadillac DeVille and an Acura RL are in roughly the same price bracket (around $50,000), but the DeVille gets top marks in the vehicle ratings while the RL is strictly a B student. Sure enough, the five-year insurance cost for the DeVille is just $4,653 according to Edmunds.com, compared to $5,083 for the RL.

How Often You Buy Cars Matters, Too

Too many people compound their vehicular overspending by trading in their cars for newer models too often. To illustrate how much of a difference it can make to trade in cars less frequently, let's use the example of twins Jordan and Morgan.

Jordan and Morgan each buy their first new car on their 25th birthday. Both borrow $20,000 for the purchase and pay off the loans over five years at 6% interest.

As soon as her car is paid for, Jordan buys another one—a pattern she continues throughout her life, until she buys her last car at age 75. We'll assume that each car is 15% more expensive than the last, reflecting average annual inflation of about 3%.

With those assumptions, Table 7.2 shows that Jordan pays nearly half a million dollars for cars over her lifetime.

Table 7.2   *Jordan's Lifetime Car Purchases*

	Loan Amount	Monthly Payment	Total Paid
Year 1	$20,000	$387	$23,199
Year 6	$23,000	$445	$26,679
Year 11	$26,450	$511	$30,681
Year 16	$30,418	$588	$35,284
Year 21	$34,980	$676	$40,576
Year 26	$40,227	$778	$46,662
Year 31	$46,261	$894	$53,661
Year 36	$53,200	$1,029	$61,710
Year 41	$61,180	$1,183	$70,967
Year 46	$70,358	$1,360	$81,613
Total Paid	$471,032		

Morgan, by contrast, keeps driving her cars for another five years after the loans are paid off. She buys half as many cars over her lifetime as Jordan—and saves an impressive $251,972 (see Table 7.3). Think about that: Just by driving her cars a few years longer, Morgan saves *a quarter-million dollars* over her lifetime.

Table 7.3   *Morgan's Lifetime Car Purchases*

	Loan Amount	Monthly Payment	Total Paid
Year 1	$20,000	$387	$23,220
Year 11	$26,450	$511	$30,660
Year 21	$34,980	$676	$40,560
Year 31	$46,261	$894	$53,640
Year 41	$61,180	$1,183	$70,980
Total Paid	$219,060		
Total Saved Compared to Jordan		$251,972	

And that's just the start of the ways Morgan could be financially way ahead of her sister.

Instead of getting loans to finance her purchases, Morgan could simply save the money that would have gone to monthly payments in the five-year period after she paid off each loan. If she got a decent return on her savings— say, 4% or 5%—and saved a little extra on the side, she could easily pay cash for her next car. If she did that with every car after her first one, she could save another $26,000 or so in interest costs she wouldn't have to pay over her lifetime.

Better yet, let's figure a money-savvy person like Morgan would take those monthly payments and invest them instead.

We'll assume that once she gets her loan paid off, she invests a monthly amount equal to what her sister is paying for a new car. We'll also assume she gets an average annual return of 8%, which is a reasonable estimate for a portfolio that's invested largely in stocks.

Once again, the awesome power of compound returns is apparent: Morgan could have a nest egg worth $2.5 million by the end, as shown in Table 7.4.

Table 7.4   *Morgan's Total Savings*

	Monthly Investment	Total at End of Five Years	Total by Year 50
Year 6	$445	$32,697	$1,091,821
Year 16	$588	$43,204	$649,957
Year 26	$778	$57,165	$387,444
Year 36	$1,029	$75,608	$230,868
Year 46	$1,360	$99,929	$137,469
Grand Total	$2,497,559		

Obviously, we're making a lot of assumptions here. The key ones are that Morgan is disciplined enough to invest the money in the years that she doesn't have a car payment and that her investments earn a higher return on average (8%) than the cost of her car loans (6%).

Of course, few things are guaranteed in the world of finance. Conservative investors who don't think they can get better returns on their money might well chose the route of paying cash for their cars, rather than getting a loan and investing their money for a potentially higher return.

The Proper Role of Cars in Our Spending

Now that you've digested all that, you can better understand why it's so difficult to answer the following question:

"I recently graduated from college and want to set up a budget. I'm trying to decide how much I can afford to buy a car. Do you have any rules of thumb?"

Well, no, unfortunately. There's really no good guideline for auto purchases, as there is for housing costs, which generally shouldn't exceed 25% of your gross income.

Some debt counselors suggest that you keep your total debt load to 35% to 40% of your gross income. (Most include housing costs in that figure, even if you're renting rather than paying a mortgage.)

The problem with that advice is that it focuses too much on monthly payments rather than on the overall cost of your debts. Someone who was paying the minimums on her credit cards, or who compressed her auto payments by taking out a seven-year loan, might be within the guidelines, while someone who pays off credit cards in full or who took a shorter-term loan might not be.

You can pretty much assume that if you're paying only the minimums on your cards, have a car loan that's longer than four years, and have a debt total still exceeding the 40% mark, you've taken on too much. But beyond that, how much of your income you choose to spend on a car is a very personal choice.

If you're a car buff, you might be more than willing to shoulder the extra costs of buying the cars you want and/or trading them in as frequently as you can.

I just ask that you look at the total amount you're shelling out for your wheels and see how that compares to your other spending and your goals.

If you're saving prodigiously for retirement, have all your other important financial bases covered, and still have big bucks to spend on cars, more power to you. The point of earning and having money is to spend it on the things that are most important to us. You might well decide you'd rather own a great car than spend your money on vacations or nicer clothes or whatever.

But if you're shortchanging other areas of your financial life or you're going deep into debt to fuel your car obsession, think seriously about the long-term costs you're incurring. As one of my finance professors once said, "Is it worth it to drive a Mercedes now if you have to take a bus when you're 70?"

You should be asking similar questions if you're considering leasing a car rather than buying.

The lease-versus-buy choice is one of those things that financially-minded types love to debate. I'll cut to the chase: If you trade in your cars every two or three years, leasing can make sense—particularly if you invest the money you save on your monthly payments.

But again, I'd recast the whole discussion. Look at the total amount you're spending on cars over your lifetime. Now compare that amount with what you're spending on other important areas of your life, including housing, vacations, education, and retirement savings.

I think most people are better off buying moderately-priced cars, preferably used, and driving them until the wheels fall off. Having a new car every few years is quite a luxury, and one that shouldn't be purchased at the expense of everything else.

Ways to Keep Costs Down

If you're convinced that you've got better things to do with your money than spend a fortune on metal, rubber, and a few computer chips, consider the following ways to curb your transportation costs:

Don't walk into a dealership if you still owe money on a car. You might as well just tattoo the word "sucker" on your forehead. Owing money on your trade-in shows you're a financial novice who's easily exploited—plus you'll get stuck with a higher-than-average interest rate on any car you buy.

Know the real cost of a car before you buy. The Internet is full of car-pricing services like Kelley Blue Book (www.kbb.com), Cars.com, and Edmunds.com that can help you assess how much to pay for a car. But you should also check out the costs of insurance and repairs. Edmunds.com's free True Cost to Own feature gives you some estimates. Many buyers also swear by *Consumer Reports'* Auto Price Service, which offers research and suggested prices for most car models (starting at about $10 per report).

Haggle smart. Knowing what the dealer paid for the car and having a firm, but realistic, offering price in mind can help you avoid the back-and-forth "Let me check with my manager" haggling that makes many people hate dealerships. Mary Butler, editor of Cars.com, says it's essential to know the dealer invoice price for any car you want, and then to add in a dealer profit of about 2% to 3%. She also recommends bringing all your research with you to show the dealership you know what you're talking about. If you're not good at face-to-face negotiations, try faxing or e-mailing dealerships in your area, telling them the make, model, and features of the car you're looking for and asking them to give you their best price. You should concentrate your efforts on high-volume, well-established dealerships that welcome virtual shoppers.

Get the right financing. If you don't have the cash to pay for a car, or if you decide you have better ways to use your money, make sure you get the best loan possible.

Your credit scores help determine your interest rate, so make sure you know what they are and what rates you can expect (see Table 7.5). (The Loan Savings Calculator at MyFico.com can give you a rough idea.) Also consider bypassing the dealership in favor of loans from credit unions or other low-cost sources, like your home equity (but read Chapter 5, "Home Equity Borrowing," first, and pay off the loan within a few years).

Table 7.5 *Auto Loan Rates by Credit Score for a Four-Year*
             $20,000 Loan

FICO Range	Interest Rate	Monthly Payment	Total Interest Paid
720–850	5.900%	$469	$2,502
700–719	6.670%	$476	$2,840
675–699	8.634%	$494	$3,723
620–674	10.778%	$515	$4,708
560–619	14.478%	$551	$6,464
500–559	N/A	N/A	N/A

Source: MyFico.com and Informa Research

There's another thing you should know: An auto loan can do wonders for your credit score if it's paid on time. So even if you have to pay a high rate now, you may be able to refinance to a lower rate in a year or so (as long as you have some equity in the car).

Buy cars that are two or three years old. Let the first driver take the depreciation hit. The cars you buy may still be under warranty, and you'll have a nice ride for a lot less.

Some people are worried that they'll get a lemon or a car that's been abused by its prior owner. But you have plenty of resources available to help you pick a good used car that you won't regret buying.

In addition to its vehicle-specific reports, *Consumer Reports* puts out an annual list of the most reliable used cars.

Before you buy a used car, get its vehicle identification number from the dashboard or doorpost and run a report from a car-tracking service like CarFax, *Consumer Guide*, or AutoCheck. These reports (which cost about $25 for unlimited searches) can help you spot a rolled-back odometer or other serious problems, like a "title wash" (which is when a car that's been in a serious accident is issued a new title in another state to try to hide its history).

A trip to a mechanic before you buy can help rule out any major problems. If you're still concerned, investigate buying a "certified" used car (but check the details of the certification program because some are better than others).

Don't agree to a loan that stretches over more than four years. In general, you should not have a loan that exceeds the life of what you're planning to buy. Specifically, you can help make sure you don't overspend on cars by paying them off within three to four years.

Longer-term loans may offer lower monthly payments, but you'll pay more over the life of the loan. If you can't afford to pay off the car within four years, you probably need to consider a less expensive vehicle.

Avoid loans with prepayment penalties. These are becoming more common, particularly if you have troubled credit. An auto loan, if paid on time, can help rehabilitate your credit score, which should in turn help you refinance to a better rate in a year or two. Lenders that want to avoid losing your lucrative business impose prepayment penalties to make it much more expensive to get out of your loan. Prepayment penalties also increase the cost if you want to try to pay off your loan early.

Try to drive the car as long as possible, but for at least a year after you've paid off the loan. Cars are better built than they've ever been, and some can rack up hundreds of thousands of miles and still not be ready for the scrap heap. If you invest money in oil changes and other appropriate maintenance, you can easily drive a car for 10 years and be money ahead.

That surprises some people, who think that once a vehicle hits a certain odometer mark the repair costs automatically skyrocket.

The reality is that even when a car does start to spend more time at the mechanic's, you still often spend less than if you took on new-car payments. The tipping point for most car owners should be reliability, not odometer readings. If you're reasonably confident your car will get you where you need to go, there may be no reason to trade it in.

If you're currently "upside down" on a car, try to "drive out" of the loan. L. R. from Houston wrote: "I have a 2002 Nissan Maxima that is in pretty good condition. Currently, I owe $21,820 on the loan but the car is worth only $12,820. I am willing to get a less expensive vehicle, used, and put some money down. What do you think I can do to get out of this car/loan?"

Trading in the car for something cheaper typically won't reduce the amount you owe and usually exposes you to a higher interest rate, since part of your loan will be unsecured debt.

If you can afford the monthly payments, the best way to cure an "underwater" car is to simply keep it until the loan is paid off. This is called "driving out of the loan." You can speed that day along by making extra payments (provided that your loan doesn't have prepayment penalties). The Houston reader might take the money she would have used for a down payment on another car, for example, and apply it to her current loan.

If you can't afford the payments, you might talk to your lender about a loan modification that reduces your monthly cost while increasing your loan term. That will raise the total cost of your car, of course, but that's usually preferable to repossession, which devastates your credit scores. (Turning in your keys voluntarily, by the way, is still considered repossession and will knock your scores for a loop.)

Also, if you're underwater, protect yourself with insurance that covers the gap between what you owe and what your car is worth. Many insurers offer guaranteed auto protection (GAP) coverage as an add-on to your regular policy, typically for a monthly premium of $10 to $25. Dealers, banks, and credit unions also offer the coverage, either as an add-on to your loan or as a one-time fee that can range from $100 to 5% of your car's value.

HOW TO REFINANCE YOUR AUTO LOAN

Katrina from Georgia had an inkling she might be able to save on her car loan, although she was looking in the wrong direction:

"My situation is I have a 1999 Hyundai Accent, and my interest rate is 23%. My credit score was around 650 the last time I checked a couple of months ago. I read about negotiating with credit card companies to see if you can get your interest rate reduced. Does that work with your loan on cars?"

Your current car lender won't knock down your rate in response to a phone call, as credit card companies often do. But you may be able to refinance to a cheaper loan.

You should check into an auto loan refinance if

- Interest rates have dropped since you bought the car.
- Your credit has improved since you bought the car.
- You got snookered when you bought the car.

Unfortunately, the last point is fairly common. An unscrupulous dealership might have stuck you with an interest rate far higher than you deserved. The difference may have even been race-based. Several studies by Vanderbilt University professor Mark Cohen found that black and Hispanic buyers were charged substantially more for their loans than white and Asian buyers with similar credit histories.

The savings for refinancing to the right rate can be substantial. At the time Katrina wrote, for example, the prevailing interest rate for people with 650 credit scores was just under 11%—or half of what she was paying.

On a $20,000 five-year loan, her payment would be about $563 a month at the higher rate. At a 10.875% rate, her payment would be $434—a savings of $129 a month.

Lots of lenders offer vehicle refinancings; credit unions often offer particularly good deals. Or try refinancing online; E-LOAN is one of the many Internet-based lenders that offer auto refinancings.

Here are some other important points you need to know:

- You need to check for prepayment penalties. If your current loan has them and they're substantial, they could offset any savings from a refinance.

- Your loan balance matters. Most lenders won't bother to refinance amounts less than $5,000; some have even higher limits.

- You need to have some equity in your car. If your vehicle is worth less than your loan, refinancing will be extremely difficult, if not impossible.

Summary

Spending too much on cars—and borrowing too much to pay for them—can wreak havoc on your financial health. One of the best ways to reduce your auto finance costs, if you don't want to pay cash for your vehicles, is to keep your loan terms relatively short and own your cars longer.

Credit Limits

- Car expenditures are a choice. There's no good rule of thumb about how much you should spend. It depends largely on how well you're meeting your other important financial goals and how important your ride is to you in relation to your other spending.

- Consider owning your cars longer. You can save hundreds of thousands of dollars over your lifetime simply by keeping your cars a few years longer before you trade them in.

- Don't walk into a dealership "upside down." Pay off the car you've got before thinking about buying the next one.

- If you can't pay it off in four years, you probably can't afford it. A five-, six-, or seven-year loan typically means that for years you'll owe more money on the car than it's worth—which increases your financial vulnerability (not to mention your overall financing costs). You definitely don't want a loan that lasts longer than you'll own the car.

Shopping Tips

- Know your credit score. Auto lending is strongly driven by scores. If you don't know yours, and the interest rates to which you're entitled, you can get stuck with a much more expensive loan.

- Do your research before buying. Save money upfront by using Internet resources and *Consumer Reports* to find the best values.

- Look into refinancing. If interest rates have dropped, your scores have improved, or you got snookered into a too-expensive loan, explore the possibility of swapping your loan for a cheaper one.

8

401(k) and Other
Retirement Plan Loans

It sounds like a great deal: Borrow from your retirement fund and pay back yourself instead of a bank. You get a great interest rate, and the loan doesn't show up on your credit report or affect your credit score.

Plenty of people take the bait. About one in five participants in large-company 401(k) plans has a loan outstanding, according to research firm Hewitt Associates. The average loan balance at the end of 2003, according to the Investment Company Institute, was $6,839.

But borrowing money from retirement plans is fraught with hazards—so many that most people should look elsewhere if they need funds. A loan or, worse yet, a withdrawal from a retirement fund typically should be a last resort, something you do only when you've run out of options.

In Chapter 2, "Your Debt Management Plan," you read about why saving money for retirement needs to be a top priority for just about everyone. Employers increasingly have shifted the burden of paying for retirement to their workers, and Social Security's future is uncertain.

The vast majority of workers should be looking for ways to *boost* what they save, rather than figuring out ways to tap their retirement funds early.

If you do decide to borrow from the money you'll need for retirement, though, be sure to read this chapter carefully so that you know what precautions to take.

Types of Plans That Offer Loans

Right off the bat, you need to know that not all retirement funds allow loans. You can't get a long-term loan from an individual retirement account (IRA) or a Roth IRA, for example. (You can take money out for up to 60 days, but if you don't put it back, it's considered an early withdrawal—which means you'll pay taxes and penalties.)

By contrast, workplace plans like 401(k)s and 403(b)s aren't *required* to allow loans, but most of them do. So do many 457 deferred compensation plans offered by government agencies.

There are some differences between these three major types of workplace plans, but all three allow workers to contribute pretax money, with their investments growing, tax-deferred, until they are withdrawn. The best-known type, the 401(k), usually is offered by a private employer, while 403(b)s are common at public schools and nonprofits. Deferred compensation or 457 plans may be offered by private employers, but they're far more common at government agencies that want to allow their workers to put aside money in addition to whatever traditional pension their jobs offer.

Many employers decide to allow loans from their plans because they know some workers won't sign up unless they can have ready access to their money. Even though loans might not be in the employees' best interest, companies know that not signing up is the greater of two evils.

Here's how the loans typically work:

- **You can withdraw up to half your balance or $50,000, whichever is less.** When figuring your balance for loan purposes, the plan looks at everything you've contributed, plus whatever employer contributions are *vested*. (Vesting means you can take that money with you if you leave your job; it's typically keyed to how long you've been with the company. Most people are fully vested or can take all their employer contributions, plus their own contributions, when they leave a job after five or six years.)

- **You're required to pay back the loan over five years.**
  Many plans allow you to take more time if the money is used
  to buy a house. Typically, the plan wants you to repay the
  money in equal installments—either that, or you can pay it
  all off in one lump sum. You typically can't speed up the payoff just by adding money to each payment.

- **You pay an interest rate that's one percentage point
  higher the prime rate.** The prime rate is the benchmark used
  for all kinds of lending, from credit cards to home equity
  loans. "Prime plus one," as lenders might say, seems like a
  pretty low rate, until you consider that these are basically no-
  risk loans. It's your money to start with, and if you default on
  a 401(k) loan, neither the plan nor your employer is out any
  cash. You're the only one who'll be poorer, since you'll owe
  taxes and penalties on the unpaid balance. Plus you'll lose
  out on those future tax-deferred returns.

The Real Cost of Retirement Plan Loans

Still, lots of people are attracted to retirement plan loans because of the low
rate and the fact that you're paying this interest to your own account. The latter feature is what leads many people to proclaim that 401(k) loans allow you
to "pay yourself back."

But are you really? Well, yes and no.

You *are* "paying yourself back" in the sense that you're not paying interest to a bank. But if you hadn't withdrawn the cash for the loan, that money
would still be invested in something in your account, and that something
probably would have been earning interest or other returns all on its own.

So instead of letting your investments earn returns, you have to dig those
returns out of your own wallet.

Some of my readers have bragged to me that they were glad they took
out 401(k) loans in 2000, when stock prices slid sharply and many people
noticed steep declines in the value of their retirement plans. At least, they
said, the money they'd borrowed was earning a steady, *positive* return, even
if it was coming out of their own pockets.

But you can't know in advance how your investments will fare over the
next five years. Many folks who borrowed against their 401(k)s when stocks
were soaring more than 20% every year in the late 1990s kicked themselves
for pulling money out of their investments to fund a loan.

Foregone returns on borrowed money aren't the only hazard of retirement plan loans. Another real problem is how quickly an innocent little loan can turn into a big tax nightmare.

Most workplace retirement plans require you to pay back a loan almost instantly if you lose your job. If you can't come up with the cash, the loan becomes a withdrawal. And that's not good.

Withdrawals are considered taxable events, which means you'll owe income taxes on that unpaid balance. If you're younger than 59 1/2, you'll also owe penalties for premature withdrawal (10% for the feds, plus whatever your state assesses). You could easily face a tax bill equal to one-third to one-half of the outstanding loan—just as your major source of income has been shut off.

Here's an example. Suppose Joe gets laid off owing $10,000 to his 401(k) plan. Since he's in the 25% federal tax bracket, he'll owe $2,500 in federal income taxes plus another $800 or so in state income taxes (he lives in California, where income taxes range up to 9.3%). The feds will want another $1,000 as a penalty for the early withdrawal, and California will take $250. In short, $4,550 of his $10,000 withdrawal—or 45.5%—will be eaten up in taxes and penalties.

Something similar can happen if you miss even one payment on your retirement plan loan. Skipped payments can trigger a default, and your unpaid balance is treated as a withdrawal.

The potential tax bill, bad as it is, is not the only thing you need to worry about. After you have withdrawn money from a workplace retirement plan, you can't put it back. The $10,000 you withdraw now could have grown to $49,268 in 20 years, $109,357 in 30 years, or an amazing *$242,734* in 40 years, assuming an 8% average annual return. So each $1 you withdraw at age 35 could cost you about $24 when you're 75.

Your money can grow thanks to the power of compounding—your returns earning returns of their own. You don't want to mess with that if you can possibly help it.

There are some exceptions to the rule that a job loss means an instant loan payback. Hewitt Associates found that 29% of large company plans allowed former employees to continue making payments on their 401(k) loans. If yours is one such company, the risks of a 401(k) loan are lessened. (If you don't have a new job to replace the one you lost, that may be tough, but at least it's easier than trying to come up with a lump sum.)

You need to consider one other issue before taking out a retirement plan loan. Is it possible that this borrowing will be a crutch to help you continue overspending? As with home equity borrowing, a retirement plan's low rate and easy terms can lead people to think they've "solved" their high-rate debt, when all they've really done is covered up the problem.

If you pull money out of your retirement plan to pay off your credit cards, and then you run up more credit card debt, you haven't solved anything. In fact, you've made matters worse. You've put your retirement at risk to pay for meals, clothes, and movies long since forgotten. You haven't figured out how to live within your means, which means you'll probably be facing another debt crisis in the not-too-distant future.

Besides, credit card debt generally is something you should be paying out of your current income. Stretching it out over five years might actually increase the debt's total cost. You may find that if you take another look at your spending, you can carve enough money out of your budget to pay off the debt much faster and without the potential disadvantages of a retirement plan loan.

If you've considered all this and you still want to go ahead, take the following steps:

- **Fix the leaks.** If you're using the money to pay off past over-spending, make sure you create—and stick to—a spending plan that prevents you from going into further debt. For the time being, at least, put away your credit cards and live on cash.

- **Check your plan's repayment policies.** You'll want to know if your loan will be called in if you lose your job or if you'll have some time to pay it off.

- **Have a Plan B.** If your company demands loan repayment when you leave your job, make sure you have some other source of cash you can tap to pay it off. Keep plenty of open space on a home equity line of credit or your credit cards, for example—enough to pay off the loan and to provide your living expenses for the several months you may need to find your next job.

- **Pull the money from your fixed-income investments.** If you have a choice, ask that the money for your loan be taken from your bond, cash, or other fixed-income investments, rather than from the stock side of your retirement plan portfolio. You don't want to miss out on the potentially higher returns that stocks can offer.

Cracking Your Nest Egg Early

If your goal is to withdraw money from your retirement plan rather than borrow it, you'll probably discover that there are several ways to crack open your nest egg.

Many 401(k)s and other workplace retirement plans allow hardship withdrawals for certain purposes: to buy a home, to prevent eviction or foreclosure, to pay medical bills, or to cover the cost of college tuition for the next year. (Your plan may allow withdrawals for other reasons, but you generally have to prove that your financial need is substantial and pressing and that you have no other resources to tap.)

Hardship withdrawals don't come cheap. They incur income taxes and can incur penalties just like any other premature withdrawal.

You can avoid the penalties if any of the following are true:

- You're 59^{1}/2 or older.

- You're 55 or older and are "separated from service," meaning that you've quit, retired, or been fired or laid off.

- You're "separated from service" and you've set up a series of regular payments based on your life expectancy. (These scheduled withdrawals, known as "substantially equal periodic payments," must continue for at least five years or until you're 59^{1}/2, whichever is later.)

- You're totally and permanently disabled.

- The withdrawal is required by a court order to give the money to an ex-spouse, child, or other dependent.

- Your medical expenses exceed 7.5% of your adjusted gross income.

The situation is much the same with a traditional IRA, although you don't have to say why you want to access your funds. You simply write a check or get the brokerage or bank holding your account to send you the money.

Again, you'll owe income taxes on the withdrawal, but you can avoid penalties in certain cases. Setting up the periodic payments just described is one way, although you don't need to be "separated from service" to do so. Also withdrawals of up to $10,000 aren't penalized if it's for the purchase of your first home.

If you're taking money out of a Roth IRA, you won't owe taxes or penalties unless the amount you're withdrawing exceeds all your previous contributions. (Any withdrawal from an IRA is presumed to be a return of those original contributions; it's not until you withdraw earnings that tax consequences are triggered.)

Just because it's possible to take money from a retirement plan doesn't mean it's a smart idea, however. In fact, it's usually the opposite.

The Hidden Cost of Withdrawals

Jim had major credit card bills—and a big IRA balance "that's just sitting there. Wouldn't it make sense to pull that money out and use it to get debt-free?"

John lost his job, and his company mailed him a check for his 401(k) balance. "I know this money is for retirement," he said, "but I need it now."

Wendy had a great idea for a business, but she couldn't convince any of the area banks to give her a loan to get started. She was convinced if she used her retirement money, the success of her future enterprise would allow her to more than replace what she took.

All these folks thought they had good reasons to raid their retirement funds. And they're all wrong.

The taxes, penalties, and lost future income I described earlier should be enough to dissuade anyone from tapping his or her retirement funds early.

But you also should realize that creditors can't touch the money in most retirement plans. It's safe in a way that other savings and assets are not. If worse comes to worst and you need to file bankruptcy, the money in your retirement plans usually can be preserved so that you don't end up impoverished in your old age.

All three of the people I described are at heightened risk of going broke. Jim's big credit card balances, John's lack of a job, and Wendy's plans to launch a business all increase their chances of financial failure, which makes it all the more important that they leave their retirement money alone.

Besides, they—and you—almost certainly have other, better options. Jim, for example, could trim his spending or get a second job to pay off his cards. John could make ends meet by getting a roommate or temporarily settling for a job that pays less. Wendy might be able to get a well-off friend to invest in her idea or get starting funds by (prudently!) tapping her credit cards.

Whatever your reason for wanting to crack open your nest egg, it's probably not good enough. *Retirement money should be left alone for retirement* except in the direst emergencies.

One of the most heartrending letters I've received in recent years came from an older couple who drained their retirement funds (and their home equity) to pay huge medical bills. They believed they should pay their own way, but the health costs proved too much for them, and they were facing bankruptcy.

What they hadn't realized is that they probably could have wiped out their medical bills in bankruptcy years earlier and spared their nest egg, which would have been protected from their creditors. Instead, they were facing a pretty dismal retirement with little but their Social Security checks to get them through.

Another move that can be fraught with peril is raiding your retirement fund to avoid foreclosure. Yes, it may help you make the payments for a while, but it also can lull you into hanging on to a house that may no longer be affordable. Sometimes it's better to sell a house rather than struggle to hold onto it; in that way you can avoid foreclosure while keeping your retirement money intact.

But what if you just want some cash for a house down payment? Or you want to retire early? Then it's okay, right?

Not necessarily. You're still giving up all those future tax-deferred gains that, if left alone, could ultimately make you a lot richer. Again, there are usually other ways to go.

In the case of a house down payment, most lenders offer mortgages with as little as 3% down. There are programs that will grant or gift down payments to certain homeowners.

When it comes to retirement, most financial planners recommend that you avoid touching your tax-deferred money for as long as possible. The typical advice is that you live off other assets until you're forced to start taking withdrawals from workplace retirement plans and traditional IRAs at age 70 1/2. That gives your money the maximum time to grow.

Frankly, you're at far more financial risk when you take funds early. Instead of having more money to fund a shorter retirement, you'll have less money to fund a longer one. With less money you have less wiggle room, and any downturn in your investments or unexpected expenses can be a disaster.

During the bear market of 2000–2001, some early retirees who had set up substantially equal periodic payments were caught in the awkward position of not having enough cash left in their IRAs to finish out their five-year withdrawal plans, let alone pay for the rest of their retirement. You don't want to get caught in that trap.

If you do decide to tap your retirement funds early, at the very least do the following:

- Have a tax pro review your plans. Some of the rules for these early withdrawals can be tricky.

- If you're retiring, meet with an objective, fee-only financial advisor to discuss your plans, your investment allocations, your withdrawal schedule, and how you'll pay for certain expenses, like health insurance. Try to start these discussions well in advance of your final day at work. Decisions about many aspects of retirement are irrevocable. You don't want to find out after the fact that you've messed up and nothing can be done.

ALL-TOO-COMMON 401(K) MISTAKES

Cashing out early is one of the worst blunders you can make, and borrowing from the plan is usually a bad idea also. But you can make plenty of other mistakes as well.

Mistake #1: Failing to sign up

Yes, there are some truly bad 401(k) plans out there, but they are pretty rare. Most participants get plenty of choices (14 investment options is typical) plus a company match.

There has been some controversy about the hidden fees companies and participants are sometimes charged for their plans. Concern about fees has prompted some employers to look for better deals. While you should encourage your employer to keep plan costs down, the amount you pay in fees is dwarfed by the value of the company match, the tax deduction, and tax-deferred compounding, so don't use that as an excuse not to participate.

Mistake #2: Cashing out when you leave your job

You're not doing yourself any favors when you let your former employer write you a check for your 401(k) balance. That's exactly how many workers blow their hard-earned retirement funds.

Four out of 10 workers cash out their 401(k) plans when they leave their jobs, according to a 2002 Hewitt Associates study. The cash-out rate is even higher among workers in their 20s, half of whom took their balance in cash rather than rolling it into an IRA or their new employer's plan.

The balances these workers have accumulated typically are small, which often leads to the attitude that these cash-outs don't really matter.

However, as you've read elsewhere in this chapter, even small amounts can grow substantially if left alone. Every $1,000 you cash out at age 25 could cost you $20,000 in future retirement money, assuming an 8% average annual return.

Plus there's the tax bill. You'll owe regular income taxes on the cash-out, as well as penalties.

If you're leaving a job and your employer won't let you keep your money in the 401(k) plan, make arrangements to roll it into an IRA. When you're old, gray, and rich, you'll thank your younger self.

Mistake #3: Failing to get the full company match

The typical large-company plan, according to Hewitt Associates, matches 50% of your contributions up to 6% of your salary. Some companies even match dollar for dollar. Your company may not be so generous, but as long as it's offering free money, you should take it.

Say your company chips in 25 cents for each dollar you contribute. Where else can you get a 25% return, risk-free, on your retirement money?

If you don't think you can afford to contribute enough to get the full match, you're probably wrong. Your contributions aren't subject to income taxes. So if you're in a combined federal and state tax bracket of 30%, each dollar you contribute reduces your paycheck by only 70 cents.

If you're skeptical, try increasing your contribution by 1% each quarter. An even more painless way to save is to boost your contribution annually by the amount of any raise you get. (If you get a 3% pay boost, just ratchet up your contribution by 3 percentage points.) You'll be glad you did.

Mistake #4: Playing it too safe

Some people are simply terrified of the stock market. Some took too many risks during the bull market of the late 1990s and then pulled back entirely when their portfolios went into freefall. In fact, about 16% of the 401(k) participants surveyed by the Employee Benefit Research Institute (EBRI) had none of their assets in stocks.

The problem with sitting on the sidelines is that you probably won't be able to achieve your retirement goals. The "safer" choices—money market accounts, guaranteed-return funds, and fixed-income accounts—typically won't give you big enough returns to offset inflation, let alone the kind of growth you'll need to retire.

Consider that inflation has been running about 3% annually, while money market funds have been paying as little as 1% to 2% in recent years. Investments in bonds and bond funds typically pay better, but they still leave you only slightly ahead of rising prices.

Most workers, regardless of their ages, need to have at least half of their 401(k) accounts invested in stocks to have adequate income in retirement.

Mistake #5: Taking too much risk

As important as stocks are to your goals, you can go too far. The EBRI study found that 30% of 401(k) investors had all or nearly all of their money in their 401(k)'s stock choices.

Most investors need the safety net of having at least some bonds and cash in their portfolio. Typically, these investments provide a cushion against the wilder ups and downs of the stock market. Folks who had their money invested in the classic balanced portfolio—60% stocks, 30% bonds, and 10% cash—got through the bear market at the turn of the century with just a few cuts and scratches. Those who were 100% in stocks got thrashed, and many made matters worse by panicking and pulling out of stocks entirely.

Mistake #6: Overdosing on company stock

Many people mistakenly believe their employer's stock is safer than a diversified mutual fund. But a single stock—even that of a company you think you know intimately—is always a bigger risk than a mutual fund that spreads its investments over a wide variety of companies.

That's why financial planners recommend that you have no more than 10% of your retirement portfolio in your own company's stock. Yet 23% of the 401(k) participants studied by EBRI had more than half of their retirement portfolios in company stock, and a frightening one in 10 had all or nearly all of their money there.

Scarily enough, the workers most likely to overdose on company stock were the ones who could least afford it: those over 60. The EBRI study found that one in seven older workers opted to put all or nearly all of their 401(k) money in company stock. One big downdraft—or, worse yet, a total wipeout like those that happened to Enron, WorldCom, and scores of other companies—could make their comfortable retirement disappear.

Summary

Borrowing money from retirement plans is fraught with so many hazards that most people should look elsewhere if they need funds. Those who do borrow money should take care that their loan doesn't turn into an inadvertent withdrawal.

Credit Limits

- Loans generally are limited to half of your balance or $50,000, whichever is less. They typically are repaid over five years at an interest rate slightly above the prime rate.

- A missed payment or a job layoff can turn the loan into a withdrawal, triggering income taxes and penalties.

- Money withdrawn from a retirement plan can't be returned, which means that every $1 you take out could potentially cost you $10 or more in lost retirement income.

Shopping Tips

- If you decide to take out a loan, fix your budget so that you're living within your means and can make the payments.

- Check with your employer about how loans are treated should you quit or lose your job; if the loan would become due, make sure you have some other source of cash to tap to pay it back.

- Ask your employer to pull the loan proceeds from the fixed-income side of your portfolio to limit the potential impact on your returns.

9

Loans You Don't Want to Get—or Give

High-rate loans were once the province of loan sharks, who worked on a fairly simple business plan: Pay us back, or we'll break your kneecaps.

Today, however, high-rate loans are big business. Four out of the 10 largest banks, for example, have payday lending arms, while the largest provider of refund anticipation loans is H&R Block. Title lenders and rent-to-own outfits can be found in most communities or quickly located on the Internet.

All are capitalizing on people's desire for quick cash, regardless of the cost. Most target low-income working people who may feel they have limited options and who often don't fully understand what they're paying for these loans. Instead of a short-term solution, these loans often spiral into a long-term problem.

Here are some of the ones you should avoid:

Payday loans. Let's say you need $100 on the 1st, but you don't get paid until the 15th. Your local payday lender is happy to give you the money—in exchange for a fee of $15 to $30. You write a postdated check for the amount you want plus the fee, and the payday lender promises not to cash your check until the 15th.

What you may not realize is that the fee you're paying for that short-term loan represents an annualized interest rate of 400% to 650%. And if you "roll over" the loan—delay repayment for another two weeks in exchange for another fee—the amount you pay for that $100 loan can quickly spiral even higher. Many people find themselves in this vicious cycle, when what they thought would be a short-term loan stretches for weeks or months because they can't pay back the original amount.

Rent-to-own deals. Whether you're buying a television, computer, or sofa, rent-to-own stores will make sure you pay a substantial premium for paying over time. A television that retails for $400, for example, might cost you 78 weekly payments of $20, or a total of $1,560. If you saved the same $20 a week for five months, you could pay for the TV in cash—clearly a much better deal.

Title or "pink slip" loans. These loans are secured by the value of your car, and you're required to hand over your title and often a spare set of keys to get the money. If you don't pay back the loan within the allotted time frame, typically 30 days, you may be allowed to "roll over" the loan—or the lender may simply take your car. Think about that: You may have borrowed only $250 or $500, but the lender may get a car worth thousands of dollars. That's why one consumer advocate has denounced such repossessions as legalized theft. The fact that you're paying annualized interest rates of 290% or more just adds insult to potential injury.

Direct-deposit advances. If you have your paycheck deposited directly into your checking account, your bank may offer the "opportunity" to borrow against your next check. These advances come at a pretty steep price, however. Wells Fargo Bank, for example, charges $2 for every $20 you borrow. If you take a week to pay back the money, that's an annualized percentage rate (APR) of over 500%; if you take the full 35 days allowed to repay, the APR's closer to 100%.

Unfortunately, as with other high-interest, short-term loans, many people don't repay on time and wind up taking out advance after advance.

Refund anticipation loans. A tax preparer fills out your return and then gives you a check on the spot (or within a couple of days) for an amount equal to your refund, "minus a few fees." Those fees can eat up as much as a third of your refund, however, and they represent another high-rate loan for a short-term debt.

You may not know this, but with electronic filing and direct deposit, you can get your tax refund within 10 to 14 days. That's what the tax pro is doing—using e-file and direct deposit to speed the money along.

So for the "privilege" of not waiting those two weeks, you pay an average of 222% on a $1,980 refund loan, according to the National Consumer Law Center, which surveyed providers of refund anticipation loans.

You'd be much smarter to pass up the loan and have your money—all of it—deposited directly into your checking account.

Pawnshop loans. Whether the cost of a pawnshop loan is outrageous or merely expensive depends in large part on the laws in your state. Some limit pawnshop interest to around 25% a year; others allow shops to charge that much per month. "Storage" and "setup" fees can increase the toll.

Pawnshops have a high rate of default: About one in five items used as loan collateral is never reclaimed. If you'll be parting permanently with the item anyway, consider selling it on eBay or to a dealer.

SURVIVING A SHORT-TERM CASH CRUNCH

Your bills are due, your bank account is running on fumes, and it's two weeks until payday. Here's how to survive without resorting to a high-rate lender:

Go on a short-term spending "diet." Closing your wallet for even a few days can help your situation enormously. Eat out of your pantry for a while, rather than buying groceries or dining out. Don't buy clothes, movie tickets, or anything else discretionary. Stop smoking or drinking for a week or two. Leave your car in the driveway and bum rides from friends. Eventually, of course, you'll have to buy groceries and return the rides (at least, if you want to keep your friends), but your short-term spending diet can give you enough cash that you won't need high-rate lenders.

Record every cent. Many people have "leaks" in their spending: small amounts that dribble out here and there, usually on impulse spending that's hard to recall afterward. These little amounts can quickly add up to pretty sizeable sums. Write down every purchase, and you'll quickly find out where that extra cash is going so that you can plug the leaks.

Raise every dollar you can. Yard sales can be a quick way to raise cash; so can selling stuff on eBay, Amazon.com, or other Internet sites. If you can, look for short-term, cash-paying jobs like babysitting, lawn care, errand running, or teaching any skill you might have. If you're overdue for a raise at work, ask. Even taking your change jar to the bank or coin-sorting machine can help you raise a little cash.

Accept help. If your financial circumstances are truly bad, you may qualify for relief from any number of sources: charities, religious organizations, your employer, your union. (The government also has plenty of programs, from welfare to food stamps, but it might take a while to qualify.) Most communities, for example, have food banks, and your employer or union might have grants or low-interest loans available.

Three More Loans to Beware

Not all questionable loans come with triple-digit interest rates. Some have APRs that seem almost reasonable. But there may still be traps aplenty:

125 or high-loan-to-value mortgages. Lenders who specialize in such loans promise to give you a mortgage or home equity loan for more than your house is worth (typically up to 125% of the home's value, which is where the loan gets its name). These loans often come with steep upfront fees (10% of the loan amount isn't uncommon) and high interest rates. Not all of the interest is deductible, since you can't write off interest on loans worth more than your house. And you'll really be in a jam if you have to sell your house for less than the mortgage; you'll still owe the difference between the sale price and your loan balance.

These loans are bad deals all around. They're costly and dangerous and use up the cushion of equity you should keep in your home.

Debt-consolidation loans. Consolidate your high-rate credit card debt into one convenient loan with a low monthly payment—and you may end up paying through the nose.

Some debt-consolidation loans do exactly what they promise: lower the total cost of your debt. But many lower your payments only because they stretch out your loan repayment term for years and years. You may wind up paying a higher interest rate on your debt, plus numerous fees that increase your costs.

"I recently was stupid and took out a personal loan at 22% to pay off my credit cards," said Charlene from Salem, New Hampshire. "Now I have a loan for 84 months that seems to be adding on more interest than I'm paying. It's hard to afford more than the minimum balance, and because I was three days late with a payment, they added on $500 in fees, including a late-payment fee, an over-the-limit fee, and finance charges. Now I just feel buried. I dug myself into a deeper hole and can't ever imagine getting myself out of it."

There's also a lot of fraud in this area, with scam artists promising loans in return for big upfront fees or commissions.

If you do consider a debt-consolidation loan, deal only with lenders you know, such as a local credit union or well-known bank. Compare the interest rate and terms to what you're paying now on the debt you hope to pay off. You shouldn't have to pay hefty upfront fees or commissions to get the loan, and you should be able to pay off the debt in a reasonable length of time.

Margin loans. Brokerages typically allow you to borrow money using your securities (stocks, bonds, mutual funds, and so on) as collateral. The interest rate you pay is relatively low—usually one to three percentage points over the prime rate—which is why some people turn to margin loans as a source of emergency cash or to fund other investments.

The big risk is that your loan can be "called" with little warning. If the value of your securities drops, the brokerage can ask you to deposit more cash in your account to bring the balance up to its minimum standards. If you don't respond quickly enough, the brokerage can seize your investments and sell them.

Inexperienced investors should steer clear of margin loans until they have a good feel for the possible swings the market can inflict on a portfolio. Even then, they should limit their borrowing to less than what a brokerage allows and have a ready source of cash to tap if their loans should be called.

ALTERNATIVES TO HIGH-RATE LOANS

If you think a payday lender or other high-rate, short-term loan is your only choice, you're probably wrong. Here are some options to consider:

Negotiate with your current creditors. If you still have good credit, you may be surprised at how easy it is to talk your credit card companies into lowering their rates. You may also be able to refinance your mortgage or auto loans to lower-rate debt and free up more cash.

If you don't have good credit, you may still be able to work out a deal. Your auto or mortgage lender may be willing to temporarily lower your payments if you're in a cash crunch.

Talk to your credit union or local community bank. Not only are community-based financial institutions typically more willing to make small loans than their larger peers, but their rates and terms are often better.

Borrow from friends and family. Yes, borrowing money strains relationships, but people you know are unlikely to charge astronomical interest rates or ruin your credit rating if you can't pay them back right away.

Consider a cash advance from your credit cards. Normally, cash advances are a lousy deal, since you typically pay a 2% to 3% fee plus a high interest rate (usually 19.9% or more). But your annual APR is still likely to be less than 100%, so if you have any room on your credit cards and your only other options would cost you two or three times as much, this might be the way to go.

"Borrow" from an IRA. If you read the preceding chapter, you know why it's a bad idea to take money from retirement funds. But if you're *absolutely sure* you can pay back the money within 60 days, you can take a "free" withdrawal from your IRA. If you're a single day late, though, you'll wind up paying taxes and penalties on the withdrawal, plus you'll lose all the tax-deferred future returns that money could have made.

Delay paying bills. Under normal circumstances, you want to pay all your bills on time to avoid late fees and possible damage to your credit score. But if your only alternative is a payday loan or other extremely high-interest debt, delaying your bill payments might be a viable option. Compare what you'd pay for a short-term loan with the late and/or over-limit fees you might incur on the bill to decide which is the better option.

If at all possible, though, try to make your bill payment within a month of its due date; many creditors report any payments more than 30 days overdue to the credit bureaus, and those late payments can really devastate your credit score.

Why You Don't Want to Cosign a Loan

So far this chapter has focused on loans you don't want to get. But there are loans you should avoid giving as well.

You may not think you're lending anything when you cosign a loan for someone else. But while you're not putting up any cash, you are lending your good name—and that may come back to haunt you. Read what happened to Doug in Ohio:

"I was the cosigner on a vehicle for my sister-in-law. I got the whole 'You're the only one who can help me,' 'If I don't have a car, I can't get to work, then I can't pay my bills...' and so on. Being soft-hearted, I gave in and cosigned for her. To make a long story short, she defaulted on the payments, had the vehicle voluntarily repossessed, and is currently filing bankruptcy on the balance, which is about $18,000. I by no means have the resources to pay for the defaulted portion, so I am in the process [of filing for bankruptcy too]. I already have two vehicles, a rent payment, insurance, a wife who is not working, and a four-year-old daughter. My credit rating before this incident was flawless, and I scored around 850. Now, from my most recent report, about a year ago, it's at 650. I am so bummed out."

Many people who cosign a loan are surprised to learn that legally they're just as responsible for making the payments as the other borrower. Late payments or defaults wind up on both parties' credit reports, and either party can be sued for repayment.

If someone asks you to cosign a loan, she probably has either bad credit or no credit. This means that, even in today's easy-lending environment, either no lender is willing to take a chance on this person, or the lenders that are want to charge sky-high interest rates to reflect this borrower's risk of default. If lenders have such a poor opinion of this borrower, you should think hard about whether you want to put your good credit rating in her hands.

Table 9.1 shows the chances that a borrower will default based on her credit score. The chance that someone with a FICO score of 800 or above won't pay her bill is just 1%, while someone in the 600 to 649 range is expected to default almost one-third of the time. Below 500, the chances of default rise to 83%.

Table 9.1   *The Risk of Default*

FICO Score	Default Risk
800+	1%
750–799	2%
700–749	5%
650–699	15%
600–649	31%
550–599	52%
500–549	72%
Up to 499	83%

Source: Fair Isaac

You may still decide to go ahead. Cosigning a loan can be a way to help a trusted young person build her credit history, or you may be helping someone who's trying to recover after a credit disaster. Whatever your reason, take the following precautions:

- **Don't sign if you can't afford to pay off the loan yourself.** Picture the worst-case scenario: Your coborrower on a car loan skips town, for example, leaving you with the debt but no vehicle to sell to help pay off the loan. If you couldn't make the payments, don't cosign the loan.

- **Don't sign if you don't have control over the payments.** The lender isn't required to notify you if your coborrower falls behind, so by the time you know there's trouble, your credit's probably already been trashed. Make sure that the loan statements and payment coupons are sent to you so that you can monitor the loan. Your coborrower can send the checks to you, and you can forward them to the lender. A hassle? Yes, but it's a small price to pay to protect your credit.

The Right Way to Make a Personal Loan

Loans between friends and family members are actually pretty big business: the World Bank estimates that such borrowing totals about $300 billion a year, and the borrowed money provides as much as 41% of personal income in some developing countries.

But the way many people lend money to family and friends is far from businesslike. Often, there's no discussion of interest rates, repayment terms, or the consequences of default. Frequently, what started as a loan turns into an involuntary gift when the lender fails to pay back the money.

Even when payments are made on time, the loan can strain the relationship. The lender might start questioning every purchase the borrower makes, with an eye to whether there will be enough money to make the next loan payment. The borrower picks up on the lender's monitoring and resents the fact that he's being judged.

This brew of ill feeling is why many people are dead set against mixing relationships and money. But private loans among friends or family members can have positive effects as well. They can help people buy homes, start businesses, or pay off high-rate debt.

The difference between a loan that's successful and one that's a disaster often has a lot to do with how much preparation the parties did up front. Consider the following questions:

Are you lending money you can't afford to lose? As one of my readers put it, "You should always be prepared for your loan to be a gift. If you get paid back, that's just gravy."

The person asking you for money is probably a worse-than-average risk. If he weren't, he'd be able to get plenty of low-rate debt from a mainstream lender and wouldn't need to bother you.

Whatever your relationship to the borrower, his need for cash isn't more important than your financial survival. If you can't afford to say good-bye to this money, don't lend it.

How will this loan affect our relationship? Ask yourself how you would feel if the borrower immediately took off on an expensive vacation after accepting your money. If your blood pressure just went up a few notches, you might want to rethink the loan. You won't be able to control what he does with the money after you make the loan.

Are you enabling or helping? "Helping" implies you're giving someone a boost to a better life. A loan that allows someone to buy a house, start a business, or get an education is often such a "hand up," rather than a handout.

Enabling, on the other hand, just allows the other party to continue the destructive behavior that got him into trouble in the first place. Any money lent to an addict, alcoholic, or compulsive gambler is almost certainly enabling (unless he's in recovery). So, too, is a loan to someone who spends compulsively, repeatedly runs up credit card debt or "underearns"—a term used to describe people who settle for low-wage jobs when their skills and experience qualify them for much better-paying posts.

Have you consulted a tax pro? Any interest you charge will be taxed as income. But failing to charge interest, or not charging enough interest, can cause tax problems too, especially when you lend money to relatives. The IRS may "impute" the amount of interest it thinks you should have charged and tax you on that. Also, any part of the loan you forgive can be considered taxable income to the borrower.

There are ways around these tax headaches, but you'll want a tax pro's guidance if the loan is for more than $10,000 or your family has made other gifts or loans recently.

Do you have a contract? It's a good idea to formalize any personal loan with a written contract that lays out the dollar amount of payments, the interest rate, the due date, and the penalties for late payments or defaults. Make sure both sides have signed and dated copies.

This will eliminate any confusion about whether this is, in fact, a loan and not a gift; the paperwork could also come in handy if the borrower defaults and you want to take a tax deduction for the loss. (Which isn't easy, by the way, so consult a tax pro for details.)

Do you want to get a third party involved? A company called CircleLending in Cambridge, Massachusetts, has created a niche market in "servicing" loans between family members and friends.

For a $199 setup fee and $9 a month, the company collects loan payments from borrowers and deposits the money in lenders' bank accounts. One mother told me she liked the fact that she didn't have to be the loan "cop." Her daughter—the borrower—confessed that having a third party involved made it much tougher to justify skipping a payment.

For a higher setup fee—$599—CircleLending will set up and record a mortgage loan with the county clerk's office. Recording a mortgage allows the borrower to deduct interest payments made on the loan and gives the lender an option for getting the money back if the borrower defaults. (Of course, you'd have to be willing to foreclose to get your cash; if the defaulted loan didn't end the relationship, a foreclosure certainly would.)

You don't need to hire CircleLending to record a mortgage; your county clerk's office should have information on how to record a mortgage debt, although many people hire an attorney to do so.

CircleLending also offers the opportunity to report the loan and its payment history to one of the three major credit bureaus. This can help borrowers build or rebuild their credit scores—or serve as a potential deterrent to those who might be tempted to default.

Summary

High-rate loans prey on consumers in a cash crunch, but there are usually good alternatives that will help you survive the crisis and keep more of your money in your pocket. You should also be wary of cosigning a loan or lending money to family or friends.

Credit Limits

- Don't start the short-term loan cycle. Payday and other short-term lenders like to argue that they're providing a popular "service" to cash-strapped borrowers. But the price borrowers pay to be serviced is simply too high. There are always other alternatives, including simply doing without the cash.

- Consider your alternatives. Cutting spending, raising extra cash, and negotiating with your creditors are better solutions than most high-rate loans.

- If you're the lender rather than the borrower, consider the worst-case scenario. If you cosign a loan, late payments and defaults will show up on your credit report. If you do lend a friend or family member money, you should be prepared not to be repaid.

Shopping Tips

- Weigh all the costs of any loan. Lenders are required to disclose the APR of loans, as well as any fees involved. With this information, you can compare the costs of different kinds of loans so that you can pick the best alternative.

- Do the math. You can find the true cost of any loan by multiplying your monthly payments by the total number of payments and then adding in any upfront or back-end fees.

10

Dealing with a Debt Crisis

Sometimes the signs of debt crisis are pretty obvious: Collection agencies are calling you night and day, or your car's been taken by the repo man, or your stuff is piled in the street because you've just been evicted.

But there were probably plenty of warning signs along the way. If you're experiencing any of the following, you're facing a debt crisis:

- You pay only the minimums—or less—on your credit cards and other bills.

- You're borrowing from one card or credit account to pay another.

- You can pay your bills only because you're draining your savings or retirement accounts.

- You're near the limit or maxed out on all or most of your credit cards.

- You're charging a larger amount each month than you're paying off.

- Your income is shrinking but your credit card balances are growing.

- You're using credit to pay for essentials like food, rent, or gas, and you can't pay the bill in full each month.

- You're using payday lenders or other high-rate, short-term loans.

- You're lying to your partner about your debt or fighting a lot about what you owe.

Angela and her husband make good money—about $60,000 each annually. But they also have $37,000 in credit card debt that's accruing interest at about 18% a year. Lately, they've found that they can't pay more than the minimum amounts due on each card.

"We don't make any late payments," Angela said, "but we also don't have any free money every month."

Their situation is almost certain to get worse. Credit card companies view borrowers who pay only the minimum as risky, and many respond by raising their interest rates—which, of course, makes it even harder for overextended borrowers to make their payments.

Even if their interest rates stay the same, Angela and her husband are likely to face some financial setback—a car repair, reduced hours at work, an accident or illness—that will upset their overloaded applecart.

It's human to want to hope for the best—that your unemployed spouse will land a job tomorrow, that your boss will give you that raise, that next month your expenses will be a bit lower so you can get ahead. You might even be dreaming that a timely inheritance or a big lottery win will bail you out of your predicament.

But wishing and dreaming won't make it so. Debt problems don't get better on their own, and usually they get much, much worse. The more your situation deteriorates, the fewer good options you'll have left.

So whether the crisis is here, or just on its way, it's important to take action now.

Dealing with Your Creditors

Go back to Chapter 2, "Your Debt Management Plan," and the section titled "If You're Already Drowning." If you haven't done so already, go through the exercises of identifying and prioritizing your bills, matching your resources with your debts, and figuring out a tentative game plan.

You'll want to do this work before you pick up the phone to talk to any of your creditors. Otherwise, you're at risk of being manipulated by the pushiest or most unpleasant lender. Knowing your priorities and resources is essential to crafting an effective debt crisis plan.

Also you need to be realistic about what debts you can pay and what debts you can't. If you're going to default on your credit cards or file bankruptcy, for example, there may be no point in talking to those creditors.

If you *can* pay, by contrast, staying in touch with creditors can help you preserve your options, as you'll soon see.

Here's what you need to know about approaching various kinds of lenders:

Mortgage lenders. Fortunately, banks and other home lenders are much better today about helping distressed borrowers than in previous generations. If you're behind on a payment or two, for example, many will allow you to catch up over the next six months so you can avoid foreclosure. Some may suspend payments or charge you interest only for a while. These agreements are usually called "mortgage workouts."

If you have sufficient income, you also might be able to refinance your mortgage to lower your payments. Just be wary of loans that might leave you worse off in the future, such as interest-only loans or those that have low teaser rates that quickly expire. Review the information in Chapter 4, "Mortgages," before you proceed.

To get any of these options, you need to contact your lenders and be honest about your financial situation. If you don't contact them and don't pay, they typically will start foreclosure proceedings that will cost you your home. If you do manage to stop the foreclosure, you'll owe stiff penalties and fees.

Again, be realistic. If your financial situation is unlikely to get better anytime soon, even the most generous workout might not help you keep your home and could leave you worse off. Many lenders, for example, add the unpaid amount of any skipped or reduced payment to the principal of your loan. If your mortgage balance keeps rising because of unmade payments, you're losing precious equity. It's typically much better to sell an unaffordable house while you still have some equity and (hopefully) an intact credit rating than to lose it to foreclosure.

If you no longer have equity in your house, consider trying to arrange a "short sale" that will allow you to get out from under the mortgage. The lender agrees to accept the proceeds of a sale as settlement of what you owe and agrees not to pursue you for the balance. Another alternative is simply turning over your home to the bank, formally known as a "deed in lieu of foreclosure." Either of these alternatives can damage your credit, however, so you want to try to negotiate an agreement with the lender that it won't report this information to the credit bureaus. After all, you are saving the lender the hassles of foreclosure.

Auto lenders. Many people are shocked by how quickly a lender can repossess a car. Typically, you need to be only a day late with your payment for repossession to become a possibility.

If you've missed a payment or two and you want to try to keep your car, calling the lender can help stave off repossession. The lender may agree to an extension or even a refinance that could lower the payments. Some aren't that flexible, though, which is why you may need to put off other bills in favor of making your car payments if money is tight (and you need the wheels to get to your job).

If you can't make the payments, frankly, your options are grim. If you owe more than the car is worth, the lender may not only repossess the car but sue you for the unpaid balance. (This is also typically true if you try to cancel an auto lease prematurely.) That's why some people try to buy time by hiding their car—either swapping vehicles with a friend who lives out of state or parking it blocks or miles away from their home and business.

If you're fortunate enough to owe less on the car than it's worth, you may want to sell it and buy something cheaper.

Student loan lenders. An official for Sallie Mae, the nation's largest student lender, once told me that student loans are "the most consumer-friendly that's out there"—and for the most part, he's right.

Federal student loans (which are guaranteed by the government, even if they're offered through private lenders) typically offer borrowers a large array of payment options:

- Temporary suspension of payments (known as deferment or forbearance) if the borrower becomes unemployed or suffers financial hardship

- Partial payments under the same circumstances if the borrower can pay some but not all of what's owed

- Various repayment options, including "income-sensitive" payments that depend on salary, and graduated payments that start small and rise over time

- Consolidation, which can stretch out repayment terms to 30 years or more and significantly lower monthly payments

- Loan rehabilitation, which expunges negative information from the borrower's credit report after 12 consecutive monthly payments are made

Even private student loans, which now make up about 20% of new loans granted to students, allow forbearance, deferment, and consolidation, which can lower monthly costs.

If you ignore these options and default, however, you may be opening yourself to collection actions by some of the harshest and most efficient collectors in the world.

Sallie Mae has purchased several collection agencies to help it go after unpaid student loan debts and is now the nation's largest collector. The U.S. Department of Education has a stable of 12 private collection companies that have reaped billions of overdue loan payments in recent years. No longer is it easy, or perhaps even possible, to walk away from student loan debt without consequences, as was common in the 1980s.

Student loan collectors typically use state-of-the-art methods to help track down defaulters and identify the best ways to get them to pay. It's routine, for example, for collectors to monitor your credit report so that they can see if your financial prospects are improving—and then they can swoop in for their share.

If the lenders can't get you to pay within a certain period of time (typically five to six years), your account may be turned over to the U.S. Department of Education. The collection agencies that work for the education department have weapons that their competitors envy, including the ability to garnish wages and seize tax returns without a court order.

You can see why it is smart to contact your lenders long before collection is even a possibility. If you're having trouble paying your loans, chances are good that you can work out some kind of repayment plan that meets your needs.

The IRS and other tax authorities. Like the U.S. Department of Education, the IRS has vast and efficient powers to collect the money you owe. The federal tax agency can garnish wages, seize tax refunds, and put liens on your property to ensure it gets its money. State and local governments often have similar powers and may be in an even bigger hurry to use them. (In California, for example, many tax pros negotiate first with the state's Franchise Tax Board when a client is delinquent, only afterward moving on to talks with the IRS, which tends to move more slowly than the state.)

The good news is that you have some options. Most people who owe $25,000 or less, for instance, can set up an installment plan that allows them to pay their IRS bill over time. If the amount you owe is larger or you can't pay it all, you can try making an "offer in compromise"—basically a settlement offer for less than you owe. Unfortunately, these offers are tricky to make and often languish at the IRS for months, so you'll probably want to hire a tax pro who's experienced in making offers that succeed.

Other tax authorities typically have similar programs and options.

Some old tax debt can be erased in bankruptcy. This, too, is a complicated area in which you'll probably need some professional guidance.

Medical providers. Another area where collections activity has really increased is the realm of doctor and hospital bills. Collectors often go after uninsured patients with a vengeance, and insurance disputes are often "resolved" by turning to collection agencies when a patient refuses to pay.

Your first line of defense is making sure your bills are accurate. Many, if not most, hospital bills contain costly errors that you can challenge to reduce your bill. Also stay on top of any bill improperly rejected by your insurer; you may need to make daily calls or enlist the help of your state insurance regulator to get the problem straightened out.

You also should explore alternative payment arrangements. Many hospitals have a "charity" budget that pays the bills of financially-strapped patients who apply. Others will arrange installment plans, waive late fees, or reduce the total amount owed in return for lump-sum payments. Many doctors also are flexible with their patients who are having temporary financial difficulties.

If you want to continue seeing a particular doctor—your child has asthma, for example, and you want her to continue having access to a particular pediatrician—it makes sense to make your payments to that doctor a priority.

If at all possible, you want to work out some arrangement before your account is turned over to a collection agency. Your credit will be damaged by the collection account, and you'll probably find yourself with fewer options for repayment. You might also be sued over the unpaid bill, which could lead to wage garnishment and other unpleasant collection actions.

Also remember that medical bills are among the unsecured debts that can be wiped out in bankruptcy. (That's also true of most legal bills and bills for other professional services, like those provided by an accountant.) If your finances are headed down that rocky road, you may well decide to conserve whatever cash you have rather than making pointless payments toward your medical bills.

Credit card issuers. Here's where your credit history and habits can have a huge influence on your available options.

Let's say you owe $10,000 on your credit cards, but you've never paid late, you've always paid more than the minimum required, and you still have plenty of "headroom" on your cards (in other words, you're nowhere close to being maxed out). Without mentioning your current financial difficulties, you could simply call your credit card companies and ask them for a lower interest rate. Since you likely have a good credit score, the issuer will probably assume you're getting other low-rate offers and will quickly agree to your request.

Let's say you owe that same $10,000, but you're using almost every available dollar of your credit limits, you've made only minimum payments recently, and you've even been late once or twice in the recent past. Not only will your issuer be unlikely to lower your rates, but on reviewing your credit situation it may decide you've become a bigger risk and decide to *raise* them.

It may seem unfair and even counterproductive, but that's how the modern credit world often works.

Policies vary by credit card issuer. Some work with troubled borrowers to waive interest rates and create an affordable repayment plan.

In fact, some will even "re-age" your debt. I'm not talking about the illegal kind of re-aging, where a collector changes the date of a delinquency to make it more recent and keep it on your credit report longer.

The kind of re-aging I'm referring to is actually beneficial to consumers. In exchange for your making a certain number of on-time payments, the creditor agrees to remove negative information from your credit bureau file. If this option is available and you can make the payments, grab it.

If your credit card company isn't interested in working with you, you might want to consider enrolling in a debt-management plan offered by a qualifed nonprofit credit counselor. These agencies can often get your interest rate waived and set up a multiyear repayment plan.

Such plans have their downsides. As I mentioned in Chapter 2, enrollment in debt management *by itself* won't hurt your FICO credit score, but some of your creditors might report your payments as late to the credit bureaus, which can hurt your score. Other lenders may look on credit counseling as similar to Chapter 13 bankruptcy and not lend to you while you're in the program or charge you higher interest rates.

You also need to pick your counseling agency very, very carefully, as Donna's experience shows:

"I had good credit prior to turning my accounts over to this debt management program, which has since destroyed my name and credit rating in just 11 months," she wrote. "They were automatically deducting the monies out of my account on the 20th of every month [but] were not paying my bills for 20 to 24 days after receiving my money and not even paying the minimum required amount! [That] caused my creditors to report me to all three credit reporting agencies [Equifax, Experian, and TransUnion]."

That's why you'll want to check the Better Business Bureau (www.bbb.org) for complaints before signing up and make sure the agency is affiliated with the National Foundation for Credit Counseling (www.nfcc.org).

You'll want to be reasonably sure you can make the payments. If you ultimately wind up in bankruptcy, your credit card debts could be erased, and the money you paid in the meantime won't have accomplished much.

Other unsecured lenders. This includes personal loans, payday advances, and other borrowing not attached to a certain asset, like a car or a house. Lenders vary enormously in how willing they are to work with troubled borrowers. As with credit card and medical bills, you should have a good idea about whether bankruptcy is an option before you approach an unsecured lender.

Child support and alimony. If you're on the hook for these payments, you may be able to negotiate informally with your ex to lower the amount you pay. But if your ex balks, you may need to go to court to prove that your financial circumstances have deteriorated substantially. Also you typically can't get rid of the amounts you already owe, although a court may be able to grant you a repayment schedule.

WHY YOU NEED TO FEAR A JUDGMENT

If you don't pay your bills, your lenders (or a collection agency) may be able to sue you in court and get a judgment against you. Then your creditor has access to a number of powerful weapons to get its money, including garnishing your wages, cleaning out your bank accounts, and putting liens on your property.

Each state puts limitations on how many years a creditor has to sue you, and this statute of limitations (SOL) may vary by the type of debt. A creditor can continue trying to collect a debt after the statute of limitations has expired, but you can no longer be sued over the bill.

However, you can inadvertently extend these deadlines in some states by making a payment on an old debt or even by acknowledging that the debt is yours, which is why you want to be careful in your conversations with creditors.

The statute of limitations is different from the seven-year reporting limitation for most negative items on a credit report. You may have a debt still listed on your credit report that's long past your state's statute of limitations, or a debt may not be listed on your report that's still well within the SOL.

Certain debts have no statute of limitations, including student loans and some state taxes. The statute of limitations for federal tax debt is 10 years.

If the statute of limitations on a debt has expired, you might still be sued, but you can prevent a judgment by proving the debt is too old. You can also prevent a judgment if you have no income or assets that a creditor can legally take; that's known as being "judgment-proof."

You also can stop or prevent a judgment by filing for bankruptcy. Such a filing stops most collection actions in their tracks and may allow you to reduce or eliminate your debts.

Otherwise, if you've been sued but the case hasn't gone to court yet, you might try negotiating a settlement with the creditor. Being able to offer a lump sum will give you the most leverage, but your creditor may be satisfied with a payment plan.

Statutes of Limitations in Years

Each state sets limits on how long you can be sued over a debt, as shown in Table 10.1. *Oral* agreements are those that aren't made with a written contract (also known as *handshake agreements*). *Written* agreements are signed by both debtor and creditor. *Promissory* notes are written agreements that include a schedule of payments. *Open-ended accounts* include revolving lines of credit such as credit cards (in most states).

Table 10.1 *The Statute of Limitations (in Years) for Different Kinds of Agreements*

State	Oral	Written	Promissory	Open-Ended Accounts
AK	6	6	3	3
AL	6	6	6	3
AR	5	5	5	3
AZ	3	6	6	3
CA	2	4	4	4
CO	6	6	6	3
CT	3	6	6	6
DC	3	3	3	3
DE	3	3	3	4
FL	4	5	5	4
GA	4	6	6	4
HI	6	6	6	6
IA	5	10	5	5
ID	4	5	5	4
IL	5	10	10	5
IN	6	10	10	6
KS	3	5	5	3
KY	5	15	15	5
LA	10	10	10	3
MA	6	6	6	6
MD	3	3	6	3
ME	6	6	6	6
MI	6	6	6	6
MN	6	6	6	6
MO	5	10	10	5
MS	3	3	3	3
MT	3	8	8	5
NC	3	3	5	4
ND	6	6	6	6
NE	4	5	5	4
NH	3	3	6	3
NJ	6	6	6	6
NM	4	6	6	4
NV	4	6	3	4

State	Oral	Written	Promissory	Open-Ended Accounts
NY	6	6	6	6
OH	6	15	15	6
OK	3	5	5	3
OR	6	6	6	6
PA	4	6	4	6
RI	10	10	6	4
SC	3	3	3	3
SD	6	6	6	6
TN	6	4	6	6
TX	4	4	4	4
UT	4	6	6	4
VA	3	6	6	3
VT	6	6	5	4
WA	3	6	6	3
WI	6	6	10	6
WV	5	15	6	4
WY	8	10	10	8

Source: CreditInfoCenter.com

WHAT YOU NEED TO KNOW ABOUT BANKRUPTCY

Individuals typically file for bankruptcy under two chapters. Chapter 7 erases most unsecured debts such as credit cards and medical bills. Chapter 13 requires borrowers to repay at least some of their debts before erasing others. (Some unsecured debts, including student loans, child support, and recent taxes, typically can't be erased, regardless of the chapter filed.)

After three previous attempts, Congress in 2005 finally approved a bankruptcy reform package that promised to make getting Chapter 7 liquidation more difficult for some borrowers.

If you make less than the median income for your region—which is true of most Chapter 7 filers—you probably don't need to worry much about the new law. If you make more, however, you're likely to be subjected to a "means test" to determine if you can repay at least some of your debt. If the bankruptcy court determines you have the resources to pay, your Chapter 7 case can be converted into a Chapter 13 filing.

If you can make the required payments in your Chapter 13, your unpaid balances will be erased at the end of your plan. If you don't make the payments, your bankruptcy will be dismissed, and your creditors can resume their collections.

If you're considering bankruptcy as an option, you should consult with an experienced bankruptcy attorney familiar with the new law to discuss your options. (Many bankruptcy attorneys provide a free or low-cost initial consultation.) If you have a moderate to high income, you may decide that negotiating with your creditors to settle your debts is a better option.

Dealing with Collection Agencies

If you've left a bill unpaid for so long that it's been turned over to a collector, your options and choice of best tactics have changed.

No longer can you hope to elicit the creditor's interest in rehabilitating your debt and keeping you as a customer. At this point, your account typically has been "charged off"—an accounting term that means the creditor has decided that repayment is unlikely. The creditor usually takes a tax write-off for the loss and passes the account to collections.

Some creditors do their collections in-house using a special department. Others give the accounts to outside collection agencies on a "contingency" basis, which means the collector keeps a portion of what's collected. Finally, a creditor may sell its overdue accounts to a collection agency outright for pennies on the dollar. (The price drops the older the debt or the more difficult the collection is perceived to be.)

In general, in-house collectors are the most flexible and the most likely to modify how the negative account appears on your credit report if you can repay or satisfactorily settle the debt.

But if you can repay even part of your debt, you should negotiate with a collector as to how the debt will be reported to credit bureaus. Most have more flexibility than they're willing to admit to erase or minimize negative marks.

Here's what you need to keep in mind:

Don't talk until you have a plan. Collectors really aren't interested in your tales of woe; many just assume you're lying, no matter what you say. You also don't want to make a bunch of promises you can't keep, especially if the debt is still within the statute of limitations; the collector might get annoyed and decide to sue.

Fortunately, there are plenty of ways to dodge collection calls until you're ready to talk:

- Use your answering machine to screen calls or employ caller ID or distinctive-ring features so that you can let the collectors' calls go to voice mail.

- Disconnect your home phone and just use your cell phone. Cell phone numbers usually aren't public and are much tougher to track down than land lines.

- Just hang up.

More-mobile debtors make themselves harder to find by moving and not leaving a forwarding address and by getting a private mailbox for their correspondence.

You have another option: writing the collector and telling them not to contact you. Unfortunately, some collectors respond to these letters by filing a lawsuit against you to collect the money.

In any case, dodging a collector is a temporary solution at best. You'll want to come up with a plan that actually deals with the problem—and the sooner, the better.

Know your rights. Tiffany owed $2,000 on her Visa, an account that had been turned over to a law firm for collection. Then she got an unexpected call—from someone who claimed to be a sheriff.

"[He said] that if I didn't return the call from the collector (about the debt), a warrant would be issued," Tiffany said.

Of course, the call wasn't from a sheriff. Owing money typically isn't a crime, and local law enforcement doesn't issue warrants for credit card debts. *Posing* as a law enforcement officer *is* a crime, though. Unfortunately, it's such a common tactic that it is specifically prohibited by the federal Fair Debt Collection Practices Act.

The act governs what third-party collection agencies can and can't do in pursuit of a debt. It's well worth reading. It is available on several Web sites, or you can get the Federal Trade Commission's pamphlet on the issue by calling 1-877-FTC-HELP.

Here are some very common practices that are actually illegal:

- Calling you at odd hours, such as before 8 a.m. or after 9 p.m.

- Calling you repeatedly

- Calling you at work if you've made it clear that your employer doesn't allow such calls

- Telling others, such as your friends, family, or neighbors, about the debt

- Using obscene or profane language

- Threatening any action that they don't intend to take or that they are barred from taking, such as suing you over an out-of-statute debt

Collection agencies and other creditors also aren't allowed to change the date on a delinquent debt to make it appear younger than it actually is, but such illegal practices are still surprisingly widespread.

Collectors also may fail to follow the law that governs what information they are supposed to provide you. Within five days after contacting you, the collector is supposed to send you a written notice telling you how much you owe, the creditor's name, and what you must do if you believe you don't owe the money.

If you send a letter disputing the debt to the collector within 30 days of getting the written notice, the collector is required to either send you proof of the debt, such as a copy of the bill for the amount owed, or cease collection activities.

Again, violations of the laws governing debt collection are so common that some borrowers have made a pastime out of suing collectors that break the law, since consumers can collect up to $1,000 per violation in small-claims court. One of my readers, a tax preparer in Tucson, told me he collected $5,000 from collection agencies in a single year in small-claims court.

You also might consider visiting one of the many Internet message boards such as CreditBoards.com, ArtofCredit.com, CreditNet.com, and CreditInsiders.com, where battle-hardened debtors share tips and ideas for dealing with creditors. Since tactics change constantly and vary by agency, these can be an invaluable resource. Just remember that anyone can join these forums; take the advice with a grain of salt and don't rely on them for legal advice.

Negotiate hard. You'll be in the best negotiating position if you can offer a lump sum to settle the debt. But even if you can offer only payments, try to offer less than you can actually pay. You might be surprised at how quickly your collectors agree to settle.

Since settlements can really hurt your credit score, you should try hard to get some kind of concession from the collector about how the debt will be reported to the credit bureaus. Ideally, all traces of the original delinquency and subsequent collections would be deleted from your credit report. Often, though, the original creditor isn't willing to erase the late payments or charge-offs. However, you may be able press a collection agency to remove the collection action, which may help your credit.

If deletion of the collection is not possible, try to get the account reported to the bureaus "paid as agreed" or "paid" rather than "settled."

Some collectors take money from a debtor and then wind up selling the unpaid portion of the debt to another collector. Or a collector might report the unpaid portion as "forgiven debt" to the IRS—which promptly sends you a tax bill.

Dennis in Minnesota didn't know this was a possibility when he negotiated a settlement with a collection agency. He had recently found a job after an extended period of unemployment and was eager to put this debt behind him and begin rebuilding his credit.

"The debt was settled for about 50 cents on the dollar," Dennis wrote me. "A few days ago I received a notice from the IRS that I had failed to report income on my 2003 tax return. It turns out that the IRS considers the [unpaid debt to be] income. I had never considered this at the time and still cannot see how this can be considered income. But the IRS is the IRS, so I will pay the taxes that are due as soon as possible. I will also have to file an amended state tax form to finally get this matter straightened out."

If Dennis had known about the potential tax treatment of unpaid debt, he might have been able to negotiate with the collection agency not to report it to the IRS—or he could at least have put aside some cash to pay the bill.

Interestingly, some borrowers report that collection agency representatives are more willing to play ball at the end of the month. These folks are usually paid on commission and may be facing quotas, just like car salespeople.

Trust no one. Obviously, with deception so widespread, you want to be skeptical in your negotiations. Just as the collector assumes you're lying, you probably should assume the same about him or her. Some collectors will promise you just about anything in return for a payment and then renege.

Margaret thought she had a deal with the collection agency that took over her credit card debt:

"I agreed to pay the debt by sending $100 a month if they would not add any finance charges [or interest to the debt]," she wrote. "The debt started at $3,294, and after six months my debt is at $3,271, only $23 less, [even though] I've sent them $600."

You'll want to get any agreements you make with a collector *in writing and in advance* of sending any money. In fact, you should document everything about your negotiations. Keep good notes, and tape your conversations if at all possible. (In some states, it's okay to record a telephone conversation without the other party's permission, but to be safe you should tell the other party what you're doing.)

Whatever happens, don't give a creditor a postdated check or agree to automatic payments drawn from a bank account or charged to a credit card. Give collectors as little information as possible. Don't reveal bank account numbers or where you work, for example.

What if Your Creditors Won't Budge?

Barbara in Connecticut cosigned $40,000 in student loans for her son, who then had trouble finding work after college. She and her husband had their own troubles, including injuries and job losses that reduced their income substantially.

The family fell behind on its payments, and the loans were turned over to collections. Their pleas for a repayment plan they can afford have been rebuffed.

"[We] feel as if we are living in a nightmare...we tried harder than hard," Barbara wrote. "They could care less."

If your efforts to negotiate with creditors or collectors fail, consider hiring an attorney to make your case. You can get referrals from your local bar association or the National Association of Consumer Advocates at 202-452-1989 or www.naca.net.

Summary

Debt problems don't get better on their own. The sooner you take action, the more options you'll typically have to fix the situation:

- **Make a plan.** Before approaching your creditors, you need to prioritize your debts, identify your resources, and create a tentative payment plan.

- **Know your options.** Lenders' willingness to negotiate and their options for pursuing payment vary widely. Your ability to erase debts also depends on your financial situation and the type of debt.

- **Take great care in dealing with collectors.** Unfortunately, violations of the federal laws designed to protect borrowers are fairly common. You should know your rights, negotiate hard, and document every agreement in writing.

11

Putting Your Debt Management Plan into Action

Now that you know more about debts and how they can be managed intelligently, you can put together a plan to deal with your finances in the smartest way. You can get rid of your most troublesome loans while increasing your financial flexibility and building your long-term net worth.

We'll assume at this point that you can pay more than the minimum on your bills (or you suspect you can do so once you've trimmed a few expenses). If you're still struggling with your debts or being hounded by creditors, you need to go back a chapter and read about managing a debt crisis.

Once your crisis is resolved and you're back on your feet, you can get started with your long-term plan.

This program has six steps:

- **Lower your interest rates** to make your debt more affordable.

- **Track your spending** so that you know where your money goes.

- **Trim your expenses** so that you're spending on the important stuff.

- **Look for cash** to speed you toward your goals.

- **Review your priorities** so that you know what's important and what's not.

- **Create a debt management plan** that works for you.

Lower Your Interest Rates

You can speed up any debt repayment plan, or free up more cash for other goals, by getting your interest rates down. Here are some of the best places to try:

- **Credit cards.** If your credit scores are good, call your credit card issuers and ask for lower rates. You can mention other low-rate offers you've received in the mail, or check the Web sites of big issuers like MBNA, Bank of America, and Citibank for competitive offers. Alternatively, you can consider (carefully!) transferring your balances to a low-rate card. For more information, review Chapter 3, "Credit Cards."

- **Mortgages.** If rates have dropped or your credit has improved significantly since you got your loan, refinancing might lower your rate and payments. But you need to beware of "quick fix" solutions that might leave you worse off in the long run. Review the information in Chapter 4, "Mortgages."

- **Auto loans.** If you owe less on your car than it's worth, you may be able to refinance to a lower interest rate. See Chapter 7, "Auto Loans."

Another way to lower your interest costs is to transfer high-rate debt to a home equity loan or line of credit. However, you do *not* want to use this option until your spending is under control and you're sure you aren't headed for bankruptcy. Carefully review the information in Chapter 5, "Home Equity Borrowing," before you consider such a transfer.

Converting high-rate debt to a retirement plan loan is another potential, if risky, option. Review Chapter 8, "401(k) and Other Retirement Plan Loans," before you decide if this is an option for you.

Track Your Spending

Before you can decide where your money should go in the future, you need to figure out where it's going now.

We'll start with your regular bills (see Table 11.1)—what many people call "fixed" expenses (although few expenses are truly carved in stone).

Table 11.1   *Fixed Expenses*

Expense	Monthly Payment
Cable/satellite	
Car loan	
Child care	
Credit cards	
Health club	
Insurance	
Internet access	
Mortgage/rent	
Personal loans	
Phone	
Retirement savings	
Student loan	
Tuition	
Utilities	

The extra spaces are for you to enter the other monthly bills in your life, but remember that this worksheet is just a guideline. You may well create one of your own that's more or less detailed. Instead of "Utilities," you may decide to track your gas, electric, water, and garbage expenses separately, for example.

If you pay a bill annually, semiannually, or quarterly, figure out how much your total expense in that category is each year and divide by 12 to get your monthly cost. If your property taxes are $2,400 every six months, for example, you'd pay a total of $4,800 a year or $400 a month.

Vacations and holidays are other big money-drainers. Estimate how much you spent last year and divide by 12 to get your monthly figure.

Finally, don't forget to include money for car and home repairs. These expenses may not be regular, but they're certainly inevitable. If you're not sure how much to budget, look at your bills from last year and add a fudge factor of about 10%.

Once you've identified all these less-regular expenses, you'd be smart to add up the monthly costs you've calculated for them and sweep that amount into your savings account each month so that you don't have to scramble when the bills are due.

Next are your "variable" expenses. You can try to reconstruct these by looking at your credit card bills and checking account statements, but you're bound to come across a $40 ATM withdrawal here and a $20 cash expenditure there that you can't identify. Sometimes these can add up to hundreds of dollars.

A good way to track these slippery expenses is to get a small notebook and a pen and write down *every* purchase you make. (If you're married or have a partner, get the other person involved as well.)

This exercise may sound dreary, but I guarantee the results will be eye-opening. I have yet to meet anyone who tried the notebook method who wasn't surprised at how quickly those little dribs and drabs of spending add up. Do this exercise for a month, and you'll have a very good idea where the "leaks" in your wallet are.

Once a week, transfer the contents of your notebook to the worksheet shown in Table 11.2. (Make four copies so that you can have a full month's worth of variable expenses to review.) At the end of the month, examine the totals for each category.

Table 11.2 *Weekly Expenses Worksheet*

	Monday	Tuesday	Wednesday	Thursday	Friday	Saturday	Sunday
Alcohol							
Cigarettes							
Dry cleaning							
Eating out							
Entertainment							
Gasoline							
Gifts							
Groceries							
Household items							
Medical expenses							
Parking							
Personal care							
Pet supplies							
Prescriptions							
Recreation							
School supplies							
Snacks							

Once you've got your totals, the real work can begin. The first step is to compare your total monthly spending (fixed plus variable) to your take-home pay.

If you're operating at a loss (your expenses exceed your income), you obviously need to make some changes. But even if you're in the black, you'll still probably want to expand the gap between your income and your outgo to fund your debt management plan.

Creating a workable spending plan may require several attempts and lots of adjustments over time. Inevitably, you'll forget some important expense or face setbacks that will leave you scrambling. Don't give up. Just keep making tweaks until the plan really works for you.

WHAT IF MY INCOME ISN'T REGULAR?

Much budgeting advice assumes that you're paid every two weeks, like clockwork, and that you can predict your income for months in advance.

Most workers, though, experience at least some ups and downs in their monthly incomes, and sometimes the variations are pretty drastic.

You don't have to be self-employed or paid on commission for this to be an issue. If any part of your pay depends on overtime or bonuses, you may have trouble predicting your pay. You also may be vulnerable if you work for an employer that responds to slack times by slashing hours.

How to cope? The best course usually is to get your expenses down to the minimum income level you believe you can count on each year. (Retirement contributions and emergency savings should be part of these minimum expenses.) When extra money comes in, it goes toward paying down your debt, boosting your emergency funds, supplementing your retirement savings, and furthering your other goals.

What you don't want to do, if you can avoid it, is live on credit cards or home equity in the lean times. That just creates more debt that you'll have to deal with later. Also be extremely wary of expenses that increase your "overhead," or fixed expenses, like a car payment, a bigger mortgage or rent payment, or any longer-term financial commitment, that might be tough to make if your income sinks.

Trim Your Expenses

For most people, cutting expenses is a lot easier than raising their incomes (although we'll talk about that too in a bit). Name an expense, and there's probably a way to trim it.

How practical those trims are and how much money you'll save depends on your individual situation and how quickly you want to achieve your goals. Someone who's bent on early retirement may be willing to get pretty frugal to leave the rat race behind; others may want to strike a more equal balance between current and future comforts. It's up to you to decide what works for you and what doesn't, but here are some areas to look at:

Housing and utilities. Moving to cheaper digs is one option; so is getting a roommate. We also discussed refinancing as a possible solution for homeowners. But short of that, there are other ways you can lower your overall housing costs:

- Opt for higher deductibles on your homeowner's or renter's insurance.

- Challenge your property tax assessment.

- Turn down your thermostat in winter and turn it up in summer to saving heating and cooling costs.

- Do full loads of dishes or clothes, and consider hanging some clothes out to dry.

- Drop premium channels from your cable or satellite TV service, or drop the service altogether.

- Drop phone extras like call waiting or cancel your land line altogether in favor of cell phone service (or vice versa).

- Find a cheaper long distance carrier (try SaveonPhone.com or LowerMyBills.com) or switch to Internet calling if you have high-speed Internet service.

- Check to see if a bundled service (phone, high-speed Internet, and television) might save you money.

Transportation. As discussed in Chapter 7, people who really want to save money on cars buy them used and drive them until the wheels fall off (well, almost). But there are plenty of other ways to save money:

- Boost the deductibles on your auto insurance policy.

- Make sure you're getting the breaks you deserve (good driver, good student, multiple-car discounts) and that your policy accurately reflects the number of miles you drive.

- Cancel collision and comprehensive insurance on older cars.

- Investigate car pools and public transportation and ask at work about any subsidies offered for using these alternatives.

- Group your errands.

- Bike or walk as often as possible.

- Maintain your vehicles properly with regular oil and filter changes.

Food. This is a big expense for most families, and nationally the typical food budget is pretty evenly divided between eating in and eating out. You can save in both areas:

- Eat out less, and use coupons when you do.

- Pack a lunch and snacks for work.

- Make a few meatless meals each week.

- Use the weekly grocery store circulars to see what's on sale, and plan meals accordingly.

- Buy generic rather than highly-advertised brands.

- Buy fruits and vegetables in season.

- Patrol your refrigerator and freezer regularly so you can use food before it goes bad

- Give up a vice (smoking, drinking, salty snack foods).

- Avoid overpackaged and overprocessed foods.

"Convenience" foods can be especially costly, so make sure they're worth it. It takes only a few minutes and a couple dollars' worth of produce to make fruit salad, for example; buying it precut and premixed can set you back $6 a pound.

Clothing. In some areas in Africa, donated apparel from America is called "dead people's clothes" because folks there can't conceive of a society so affluent that it would toss out perfectly serviceable items. You needn't wear clothes until they're in tatters, but there may be a number of ways you can cut down on costs:

- Check out consignment and thrift stores for gently-used items.

- Know what looks good on you, and stick to classic styles rather than chasing trends. (Watch a few episodes of *What Not to Wear* if you're unclear on the concept.)

- Buy pieces that work with what you already own.

- Avoid dry-clean-only pieces.

- Solicit hand-me-downs from friends and family or hold a clothing swap with friends. (One woman's "fat pants" may be another woman's maternity outfit.)

- Give kids a clothing allowance or offer "matching funds" for what they want to buy. (Nothing encourages youthful frugality like their having to use their own money.)

You'll find lots more ideas on Web sites like the Dollar Stretcher (www.stretcher.com) or in Amy Dacyczyn's book *The Tightwad Gazette* (available at your local library—another great way to save money).

Of course, once you've sketched out a tentative budget for your expenses, you still have to stick to it. Here are some ways to avoid overspending:

- **Don't shop for recreation.** Avoid stores or malls unless you have a specific, necessary purchase to make—and then buy your item and get the heck out. Don't be lured by sales that entice you to spend more than you planned on unnecessary items; you're not saving if you spend more than you planned in the first place.

- **Use shopping lists.** Merchants spend millions of dollars a year on strategies to get you to buy on impulse. Lists are your way of fighting back. For example, I made a list of the items we commonly purchase at our favorite grocery store and organized them by aisle. (This was pretty easy to create on the computer after a few shopping trips.) I make a dozen or so printouts at a time and attach them to the side of the freezer with a magnetic clip. We check off the items we need as we run out and take the list with us when we shop. We also have a couple of blank pads (also magnetized on the back) to write down items we need at the drugstore, warehouse store, and other shops.

- **Dump catalogs.** Tracey McBride, author of *Frugal Luxuries*, discussed how leafing through glossy catalogs can give her a severe case of the "I want"s. Even if she was perfectly happy with her life a moment earlier, the images in these catalogs can spawn a yearning that can be satisfied only with yet another credit card purchase. Do yourself a favor and get off the mailing lists or simply toss catalogs in the trash.

- **Limit surfing.** If online purchases are your Achilles' heel, limit your time on the Internet. Remove your favorite shopping sites from your browser and move your computer to a more public place in your home if that's what it takes to curb your habit.

Look for Cash

We'll assume that you won't win the Powerball lottery anytime soon and that your rich aunt Dottie, dog-lover that she is, will bequeath her fortune to the Pekinese Preservation Program. So what other ways can you make ends meet?

Boost your income. Working more hours, adding a second job, or asking for a raise are all time-honored ways of earning yourself out of a financial bind or freeing up more money for debt repayment plans.

Then again, you may need to find a *better* job—particularly if you have a history of "underearning," or working for wages that are substantially less than what your education and experience should command. Some people get trapped in low-paying jobs because they really can't find anything better, but others settle for less because they lack the confidence or drive to get what they deserve. If you think that may describe your situation, you may want to explore what's holding you back and consider a support group, like Debtors' Anonymous, whose members may be dealing with similar issues.

Adjust your withholding. Keep the money that's yours rather than loaning it interest-free to Uncle Sam. Of the 120 million individual tax returns filed in 2005, 70% or 84.7 million were issued refunds that averaged $2,144. That's $178 a month that those families could have applied to other goals. You can use a calculator on the IRS Web site (www.irs.gov) to refigure your withholding so that more of your money stays in your wallet.

Consider raiding your savings. After talking about the importance of financial flexibility, now I'm trying to get you to drain that emergency fund you so painfully scraped together? In many cases, yes. For example, it makes no sense to carry high-rate credit card debt when you have cash loitering in a low-interest savings account. You can always use those cards in an emergency; meanwhile, you're not paying all that money in interest charges.

This holds true for investments you own outside your retirement funds, such as mutual funds in a brokerage account or stock options you haven't exercised. You may want to consult a tax pro about the IRS implications of selling those investments, but typically they would be put to better use paying off high-rate debt.

What might not make sense is raiding your savings to pay off low-rate debt that won't necessarily increase your financial flexibility, like student or car loans.

Sell some stuff. You may have some big stuff you can let go of, like an unneeded vehicle or jewelry that isn't heirloom (or that is, but you're willing to part with it). Even if you don't, though, chances are good you have something to sell. Perhaps lots of somethings.

The size of the average new home has nearly doubled in the past 35 years, even as families have gotten smaller. Demand for storage facilities is up 50% in recent years, according to the Self Storage Association. A whole new genre of home shows has popped up (*Clean Sweep*, *Mission: Organization*, *Life Laundry*) to help householders deal with having *too much stuff*.

So why not turn some of your clutter to cash? You can have a garage sale or explore the world of online selling.

This latter option is so popular and so effective for many people that I've devoted the next section to it.

Sell Your Surplus Stuff Online

In the bad old days—a decade or so ago—your options for selling your surplus possessions were pretty limited: yard sales, consignment shops, newspaper ads. A few Internet-savvy folks had access to online bulletin boards where they could trade their stuff, but the audience was still fairly small.

Today you can tap a massive worldwide market of potential buyers with relatively little effort. The huge success of eBay and other online "flea markets" has allowed millions of people to get top dollar for their stuff.

If you've never sold online before, getting started can seem daunting. You may have heard about spiraling fees at auction sites, problems caused by picky buyers, and even the possibility of fraud. But with a little research and a few precautions, you can prevent the most common problems and get your items sold with little hassle.

Four of the most popular sites are Amazon.com, Craigslist, eBay, and Half.com.

Each site has guides and FAQs (frequently asked questions) for newcomers, but these principles apply in general:

Research the site. Each site has its particular strengths. All four allow you to set a fixed price for your item; eBay also offers an auction feature that may land you more than you expected for your wares. (Most long-time eBay sellers have a story about an item they picked up for a song at a garage sale and then sold for a hefty profit at auction.)

Half.com is a good site for selling relatively new books, music, movies, and some electronics. So is Amazon.com, although it charges slightly more. Neither site charges for listings, which can be helpful if you're not sure your item will sell, and both have easy sign-up procedures. Craigslist, which functions like a huge classified advertising section divided by cities, has no listing or selling fees. It's often the best place to sell items you wouldn't want to ship, such as furniture and other bulky stuff. eBay, with its millions of listings and tens of millions of active users, remains the go-to site for a laundry list of items, including collectibles, jewelry, designer or formal wear, or anything weird, rare, or hard-to-find. eBay has both listing and selling fees (also called commissions).

Research your item. See what others are charging and notice the words they use to describe the item. Using the right "keywords" can lure more potential buyers. It matters a lot to collectors if your old plates are fire sale or Fire King, for example.

Sell it right. Clear pictures of your item can help it sell; so too can including all the appropriate details (such as dimensions, weight, and materials used). Be honest about the condition, since failing to do so will lead to unhappy buyers who will trash your all-important "seller feedback" ratings. If you want to sell more than one item, you need good ratings to encourage people to buy from you.

Consider costs. If your item is worth only a few bucks, a yard sale is probably a better way to sell it. Otherwise, your profit will be largely eaten up by fees, commissions, and shipping expenses or just the hassle of arranging delivery.

Stay alert. If you don't check your e-mail for days or you drag your heels on shipping the item once it's sold, buyers will complain and damage your seller ratings.

Protect yourself. Phony cashier's checks and fake escrow sites are among the ways sellers can be defrauded. Unless you complete the transaction face-to-face and insist on cash (as do many people who use Craigslist), you'll want to employ some kind of middleman. Amazon.com and Half.com collect and disburse money for their sellers, while eBay recommends using PayPal, an online payment service. If your buyer insists on using a particular escrow site, beware unless it's one of the services specifically recommended by eBay (check the eBay site under "Services" for a list). Also employ some kind of package tracking so that your buyer can't pretend the item never arrived.

You might want to explore other alternatives as well. So-called "trading assistants" can handle your eBay auctions for you; you just drop off your stuff, and they do the rest. The price is a bit steep, typically 30% or more of the final sale price, so it's an option best kept for more expensive items that you don't have time to handle yourself.

You also might look for trading forums on Web sites devoted to a specific hobby or vocation. Sites for computer buffs, for example, often contain a section where users can list items for sale. Just be sure to carefully read the rules and suggestions for newcomers before you post your item.

Review Your Priorities

Any financial plan is a juggling act of conflicting priorities and limited resources. You make only so much money (even if you add a second or third job), and your wants can be almost endless.

In earlier chapters, you read that debt repayment needs to be part of your larger financial strategy. Specifically, you need to make sure that you're taking appropriate advantage of retirement savings opportunities and that you can access sufficient funds in an emergency. You'll also want to think about your other important goals—the things you want to do, accomplish, or create for your family. As you work with your budget, you'll want to make sure that these important areas are adequately addressed and funded. If you need a refresher on these concepts, reread Chapter 2, "Your Debt Management Plan."

Also in Chapter 2, you used a worksheet to list all your debts and the relevant details, such as balances owed, interest rates, and so on. Now it's time to go back over those debts, fill in any new interest rates or payments, and assign each a repayment priority: high, medium, or low. Use Table 11.3 to do this.

These priorities are entirely up to you, based on your knowledge of your goals and current financial situation.

Paying off credit card debt should usually be a high priority. It's usually your most expensive debt, and even if you've currently got a low rate, you're limiting your financial flexibility by carrying a balance.

Auto and student loans are usually medium- to low-priority debts. Paying them off typically doesn't increase your financial flexibility much, and interest rates on these debts are usually quite reasonable. If these are your highest-rate loans, though, and you have extra money to pay them off, you might well decide to give them higher priority.

A home equity line of credit could be high-, medium-, or low-priority, depending on your circumstances. Generally, this relatively low-rate, potentially deductible debt will be far down on the payback list, but you may want to move it higher if a HELOC is your only source of emergency cash.

Paying off your mortgage, meanwhile, is usually a low priority. Generally, you should have retired all your other debts before you consider prepaying a mortgage.

Table 11.3 *Debt Repayment Worksheet*

Debt	Lender	Balance	Interest Rate	Minimum Payment	Priority	New Payment
Mortgage 1						
Mortgage 2						
Home equity line of credit						
Home equity loan						
Student loan 1						
Student loan 2						
Student loan 3						
Student loan 4						
Credit card 1						
Credit card 2						
Credit card 3						
Credit card 4						
Auto loan 1						
Auto loan 2						
Auto loan 3						
Other vehicle loan						
401(k) loan						
Personal loan 1						
Personal loan 2						

Once you've assigned priorities to your debts, you can start creating your debt repayment plan. You can use the worksheet shown in Table 11.4 to play with the numbers until you have a plan that works. After that's done, you can return to Table 11.3 and fill in the new payments you want to make toward your highest-priority debt or debts. You can use the Quicken Debt Reduction Planner I mentioned in Chapter 2 to see how long it will take you to retire each debt using your plan.

Table 11.4   *Debt Repayment Plan*

Type of Income	Monthly Amount
Wages and salary	
Extra job/hours	
Total	

Type of Expense	Monthly Payment
Fixed expenses	
Variable expenses	
Retirement	
Emergency fund	
Debt repayment	
Total	

Creating a financial plan that allows you to meet your current expenses, save for retirement, enhance your financial flexibility, and pay down your highest-priority debt isn't easy, but now you have all the information you need to get going.

Stay on Track

I wish I could promise you smooth sailing from here on out, but few of us have lives that don't throw us an occasional curveball.

Here's my best advice for how to stay on track despite whatever comes:

- **Get support.** Living a frugal or even goal-centered life isn't exactly a mainstream choice in America, where every time you turn around advertisers are shouting at you to spend more. That's why it can be helpful to find others who share your goals. You may be able to find a "simple living" support or study group in your area; start your search at www.simple-living.net. If you have a severe or uncontrollable spending problem, investigate Debtors Anonymous, which is a 12-step group based on the principles of Alcoholics Anonymous that can provide invaluable information and support.

- **Use wish lists.** If there's something you really want, write it down and stick it in a prominent place, like your refrigerator. Wait three weeks and see if the purchase is still a priority. Many times your desire for the item will have faded. (Some people put their wish lists next to a picture of their ultimate goal: a new home, perhaps, or a happy retired couple playing golf. That can help make the decision to forgo the impulse item a lot easier.)

- **Boot bad influences.** Almost inevitably, somebody in your life—perhaps many somebodies—won't understand what you're doing and may even feel threatened by it. The worst of these somebodies may actively try to undermine your attempts to reach your financial goals. For example, one of my readers described a friend who constantly invited her to expensive restaurants and concerts and determinedly rebuffed the reader's suggestions that they find more affordable entertainment. Another had a mother-in-law who kept pushing him to enroll his children in a private school the family couldn't afford, even though the public schools in their neighborhood were quite good. You may need to limit your interaction with these folks—at least until you can smile and ignore their needling.

- **Beware of quick fixes.** People who take shortcuts often find themselves not getting to their destination at all, and that's particularly true with money. Get-rich-quick schemes, high-risk investments, gambling, and even chain letters may tempt you off the slow and steady path to building wealth. Just remember that every dollar you waste on any of these bogus "solutions" is a dollar that won't get you closer to your goals.

- **Watch for signs of "frugality burnout."** Feeling deprived
  can tempt you to throw in the towel on your financial plan, so
  make sure you build occasional treats into your budget—dinner out, a movie, a little mad money to waste any way you
  want. Go ahead and buy that latte or ice cream cone or get a
  manicure now and then. If you can't afford to go away on
  vacation this year, take time off anyway and be a tourist in
  your own area. Don't put off all your rewards for the future;
  enjoy a few today as well.

- **Get back on the horse.** No matter how carefully you plan
  and how committed you are to your goals, stuff can happen.
  You can lose a job, suffer an illness, get in an accident, or be
  thrown off track in any number of ways. You may despair of
  ever reaching your goals. In fact, you might need to figure
  out a new plan or even rethink your goals. Just remember,
  winners are the ones who don't give up.

Some Final Thoughts

You've done the kind of work that creates success. You've examined your
situation with clear eyes, ascertained your goals, and created a plan to
achieve them.

As your wealth grows, you'll be able to retire even more of your debt—
but you'll also be able to add new loans when needed without anxiety or
unnecessary stress. Instead of feeling controlled by your debt, you can feel in
control of your money.

I hope you'll write to tell me about your plans, your challenges, and your
successes. Readers' stories helped shape this book, and perhaps something
you've learned along the way might be helpful to others. The best way to
reach me is through my Web site, www.lizweston.com.

Good-bye, and good luck!

INDEX

Check out...

Your Credit Score

How to Fix, Improve, and Protect the
3-Digit Number that Shapes Your Financial Future

Liz Pulliam Weston

ISBN: 0-13-148603-9
$17.95
© 2005 Pearson Education, Inc.

Here's a sneak peek at Chapter 1...

1

WHY YOUR CREDIT SCORE

MATTERS

In recent years, a simple three-digit number has become critical to your financial life.

This number, known as a credit score, is designed to predict the possibility that you won't pay your bills. Credit scores are handy for lenders, but they can have enormous repercussions for your wallet, your future, and your peace of mind.

How Your Credit Score Affects You

If your credit score is high enough, you'll qualify for a lender's best rates and terms. Your mailbox will be stuffed with low-rate offers from credit card issuers, and mortgage lenders will fight for your business. You'll get great deals on auto financing if you need a car, home loans if you want to buy or improve a house, and small business loans if you decide to start a new venture.

If your score is low or nonexistent, however, you'll enter a no-man's-land where mainstream credit is all but impossible to come by. If you find someone to lend you money, you'll pay high rates and fat fees for the privilege. A bad or even mediocre credit score easily can cost you tens of thousands and even hundreds of thousands of dollars in your lifetime.

You don't even have to have tons of credit problems to pay a price. Sometimes all it takes is a single missed payment to knock more than 100 points off your credit score and put you in a lender's high-risk category.

That would be scary enough if we were just talking about loans. But landlords and insurance companies also use credit scores to evaluate applicants. A good score can win you cheaper premiums and better apartments; a bad score can make insurance more expensive and a place to live hard to find.

Yet too many people know far too little about credit scores and how they work. Here's just a sample of the kinds of emails and letters I get every day from people puzzling over their credit:[1]

"I just closed all of my credit card accounts trying to improve my credit. Now I hear that closing accounts can actually hurt my score. How can I recover from this? Should I try to reopen accounts so that I can have a higher amount of available credit?" Hallie in Shreveport, LA

"How do you get credit if you don't have it? I keep getting turned down, and the reason is always 'insufficient credit history.' How can I get a decent credit score if I don't have credit?" Manuel in San Diego, CA

"I am a 25-year-old male who made a few bad credit decisions while in college, as many of us do. I need to improve my credit drastically so I do not continue to get my eyes poked out on interest. What can I do to boost my credit score fast?" Stephen in Dallas, TX

"I joined a credit counseling program because I was in way over my head. But my wife and I plan on buying a house within the next three years, and she has expressed concern that my participation in this debt management program could hurt my credit score. What should I do to help my overall chances with the mortgage process and get the best rate possible?" Paul in Lodi, NJ

"I'm 33 and have never had a single late payment or credit issue in my life. Yet, my credit score isn't as high as I thought it would be. What does it take to get a perfect score?" Brian in South Bend, IN

1 As with other real-life anecdotes in this book, the writers' anonymity has been protected and their messages might have been edited for clarity.

What these readers sense, and what credit experts know, is that ignorance about your credit score can cost you. Sometimes people with great scores get offered lousy loan deals but don't realize they can qualify for better terms. More often, people with bad or mediocre credit get all the loans they want, but they don't realize the high price they're paying.

What It Costs Long Term to Have a Poor or Mediocre Credit Score

If you need an example of exactly how much a credit score can matter, let's examine how these numbers affect two friends, Emily and Karen.

Both women got their first credit card in college and carried an $8,000 balance on average over the years. (Carrying a balance isn't smart financially, but unfortunately, it's an ingrained habit with many credit card users.)

Emily and Karen also bought new cars after graduation, financing their purchases with $20,000 auto loans. Every seven years, they replaced their existing cars with new ones until they bought their last vehicles at age 70.

Each bought her first home with $350,000 mortgages at age 30, and then moved up to a larger house with $450,000 mortgages after turning 40.

Neither has ever suffered the embarrassment of being rejected for a loan or turned down for a credit card.

But here the similarities end.

Emily was always careful to pay her bills on time, all the time, and typically paid more than the minimum balance owed. Lenders responded to her responsible use of credit by offering her more credit cards at good rates and terms. They also tended to increase her credit limits regularly. That allowed Emily to spread her credit card balance across several cards. All these factors helped give Emily an excellent credit score. Whenever a lender tried to raise her interest rate, she would politely threaten to transfer her balance to another card. As a result, Emily's average interest rate on her cards was 9.9 percent.

Karen, by contrast, didn't always pay on time, frequently paid only the minimum due, and tended to max out the cards that she had. That made lenders reluctant to increase her credit limits or offer her new cards. Although the two women owed the same amount on average, Karen tended to carry larger balances on fewer cards. All these factors hurt Karen's credit—not enough to prevent her from getting loans, but enough for lenders to charge her more. Karen had much less negotiating power when it came to interest rates. Her average interest rate on her credit cards was 19.9 percent.

Credit Cards

	Emily	Karen
Credit score	750	650
Interest rate	9.90%	19.90%
Annual interest costs	$792	$1,592
Lifetime interest paid	$39,600	$79,600
Karen's penalty		$40,000

Emily's careful credit use paid off with her first car loan. She got the best available rate, and she continued to do so every time she bought a new car until her last purchase at age 70. Thanks to her lower credit score, Karen's rate was three percentage points higher.

Auto Loans

	Emily	Karen
Credit score	750	650
Interest rate	5.00%	8.00%
Monthly payment	$377	$406
Interest cost per loan	$2,646	$4,332
Lifetime interest paid	$21,166	$34,653
Karen's penalty		$13,487

The differences continued when the women bought their houses. During the 10 years that the women owned their first homes, Emily paid $68,000 less in interest.

Mortgage 1 ($350,000)

	Emily	Karen
Credit score	750	650
Interest rate	5.50%	7.375%
Monthly payment	$1,987	$2,417
Total interest paid (10 years)	$174,760	$243,020
Karen's penalty		$68,261

Karen's interest penalty only grew when the two women moved up to larger houses. Over the 30-year life of their mortgages, Karen paid nearly $200,000 more in interest.

Mortgage 2 ($200,000)

	Emily	Karen
Credit score	750	650
Interest rate	5.50%	7.375%
Monthly payment	$2,555	$3,108
Total interest paid (30 years)	$469,818	$668,894
Karen's penalty		$199,894

Karen's total lifetime penalty for less-than-stellar credit? More than $320,000.

If anything, these examples underestimate the true financial cost of mediocre credit:

- The interest rates in the examples date from early 2004—a time when rates were near record lows. Higher prevailing interest rates would increase the penalty Karen pays.

- Karen probably paid insurance premiums that were 20 percent to 30 percent higher than Emily's, and she might have had more trouble finding an apartment, all because of her credit.

- The examples don't count "opportunity cost"—what Karen could have achieved financially if she weren't paying so much more interest.

Because more of Karen's paycheck went to lenders, she had less money available for other goals: vacations, a second home, college educations for her kids, and retirement.

In fact, if Karen had been able to invest the extra money she paid in interest instead of sending it to banks and credit card companies, her savings might have grown by a whopping $2 million by the time she was 70.

With so much less disposable income and financial security, you wouldn't be surprised if Karen also experienced more anxiety about money. Financial problems can take their toll in innumerable ways, from stress-related illnesses to marital problems and divorce.

So, if you've ever wondered why some families struggle while others in the same economic bracket seem to do just fine, the answers typically lie with their financial habits—including how they handle credit.

50 Ways to Protect Your Identity and Your Credit

Everything You Need to Know About Identity Theft, Credit Cards, Credit Repair, and Credit Reports

BY STEVE WEISMAN

The world of credit is fraught with peril. First, there's the enormous and growing risk of identity theft, which victimized nearly 10 million Americans in 2003 alone. But the quieter risks are just as real: inaccurate credit reports that drive up your interest rates or prevent you from getting loans, fine print in credit agreements that can cost you hundreds or even thousands of dollars, "credit repair" services that only make matters worse. In *50 Ways to Protect Your Identity and Your Credit,* consumer finance expert and nationally syndicated radio host Steve Weisman tells you exactly what to watch out for and how to keep credit disasters from happening to you. Writing in plain English, Weisman reveals how criminals gain access to your credit, bank, or brokerage accounts; open new accounts and take out loans in your name; and how to use the law, technology, and common sense to protect yourself. You'll learn how to recognize "phishing" scams and dishonest credit counselors, how to understand and eliminate the hidden costs of credit, and much more. Weisman's checklists tell you what to do right now, before you're victimized. And if you've already been attacked, Weisman presents step-by-step techniques, form letters, and affidavits you can use to help restore your credit—and your good name.

ISBN 013146759X, © 2005, 256 pp., $19.95

10 Secrets to Successful Home Buying and Selling

Using Your Housing Psychology to Make Smarter Decisions

BY LOIS A. VITT, PH.D.

Buying a home isn't just the most important financial decision you'll ever make: it's one of the most important emotional decisions, too. Get it right with *10 Secrets to Successful Home Buying and Selling.* Dr. Lois Vitt shows exactly how to go after the home that's perfect for you—with more confidence and less anxiety. You'll discover your "nesting profile": your own personal housing psychology. Buying a home with a partner or children? You'll learn how your nesting profile compares with theirs...so you can make the best decisions for all of you. Vitt illuminates every decision through practical examples, real life stories, and easy quizzes...all designed to make you aware of issues you've never considered and avoid disastrous housing mistakes.

ISBN 0131455001, © 2005, 288 pp., $17.95